# ISLAMIC
# METALWORK
## IN THE BRITISH MUSEUM

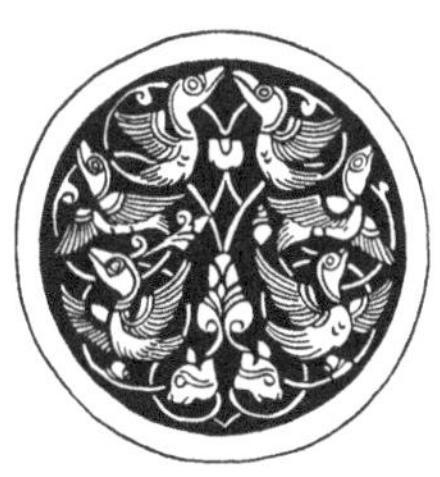

DOUGLAS BARRETT

*Assistant Keeper in the Department
of Oriental Antiquities*

*Published by
The Trustees of the British Museum
London
1949*

*Photographs by*
VICTOR FURST

# CAMBRIDGE
**UNIVERSITY PRESS**

University Printing House, Cambridge CB2 8BS, United Kingdom

Cambridge University Press is part of the University of Cambridge.

It furthers the University's mission by disseminating knowledge in the pursuit of
education, learning and research at the highest international levels of excellence.

www.cambridge.org
Information on this title: www.cambridge.org/9781107438392

© Cambridge University Press 1949

First published 1949
First paperback edition 2014

ISBN 978-1-107-43839-2 Paperback

Cambridge University Press has no responsibility for the persistence or accuracy of
URLs for external or third-party internet websites referred to in this publication,
and does not guarantee that any content on such websites is, or will remain, accurate
or appropriate.

This publication is in copyright. Subject to statutory exception
and to the provisions of relevant collective licensing agreements,
no reproduction of any part may take place without the written
permission of Cambridge University Press.

*A catalogue record for this publication is available from the British Library*

# PREFACE

Metalwork provides the most continuous and best-documented material for the history of Islamic art. Especially is this so from the beginning of the 12th century to the end of the 14th century, when pieces abound inscribed with the names of rulers of every part of the Islamic world between Egypt and India.

The greater part of the collection of Islamic metalwork was acquired by the Museum during the long Keepership of Sir Augustus Wollaston Franks, 1866–1896: but a few pieces, including the important pair of early ewers (pages ix - x) were acquired earlier, while in this century gaps have been filled as occasion has offered. The collection is now reasonably representative and includes a number of pieces of first-class importance. It therefore deserves to be better known than it is. Three collections in particular have contributed to it: that of the Duc de Blacas (1770–1839), Royalist, diplomat and connoisseur, of John Henderson (d. 1878) antiquary and collector, and of William Burges (1827–1881) architect and designer. The first was dispersed by auction in Paris in 1866 when the Museum acquired twenty-one pieces; the other two collections, rich in many other respects also, were bequeathed to the Museum on the deaths of their owners.

In 1886 Stanley Lane-Poole published descriptions of a number of the more important pieces of Islamic metalwork then in the Museum in his *Art of the Saracens in Egypt*, but this work was illustrated only by a few woodcuts. More recently about a dozen pieces from the collection figure among the illustrations to Migeon's *Manuel* and a like number in the plates accompanying Mr. R. Harari's article on Metalwork in *The Survey of Persian Art*. It will be seen that the present book is the first attempt to treat the collection as a whole; the illustrations are all from new photographs especially taken for it. The text, which has been written by Mr. D. E. Barrett, Assistant Keeper in the Department, gives a survey of the history of the subject with references to pieces in the collection and to the most important examples elsewhere.

Only the subjects reproduced have been described in detail, but they have been chosen to illustrate, so far as possible, every phase of the subject while including all the finest pieces in the Museum collection. The dish shown on Plate 1 is at present in the Department of Egyptian and Assyrian Antiquities; the remainder are all in the Department of Oriental Antiquities. The metalwork in Islamic style, made in Venice, has not been included: a number of good examples are in the Department of British and Medieval Antiquities of the Museum.

Basil Gray
*Keeper of Oriental Antiquities*

July 1949

iii

# INTRODUCTION

In 622, the first year of the Muhammadan era, the prophet Muhammad fled from Mecca to Medina with a few followers. A hundred years later the temporal power of Islam extended from Spain in the west to Western Turkestan and Sind in the east. The contribution of the Arabs to the culture of this vast empire was threefold: the religion of Islam and a magnificent language and script. For the rest they drew on the ancient civilizations of the countries which they overran. The Umayyad caliphs or successors of the prophet, who ruled the Islamic world from 661 to 749, transferred the capital to Damascus in Syria. To embellish it they made use of Egyptian, Syrian, and Byzantine craftsmen. Fine metalwork was made in both Syria and Egypt during the first six centuries of our era, and much of the silver treasure found throughout the Roman Empire, of which the Esquiline and Mildenhall Treasures in the Museum are good examples, was probably made in the Eastern Mediterranean area, at Antioch or Alexandria. Bronzework was practised by the Copts, the Christians of Egypt, who used forms, like the standing-lamp and the incense-burner, which were adopted and developed by the metalworkers of the Near East during the Islamic period.

## PERSIA, 7TH TO 13TH CENTURY

In 749, a revolt in Eastern Persia overthrew the Umayyads, and the Abbasids, who succeeded, moved the capital from Damascus to Baghdad. The rapidly increasing influence of Persian art on the formation and development of the Islamic style dates from this period. The Sasanians (226–642), the native Persian dynasty overthrown by the Arabs, had been responsible for some remarkable metalwork. Their ewers, cups and bowls in gold, silver, silver-gilt and bronze rank among the finest plate ever made. Every technique – casting, carving, engraving, repoussé work, and niello – was freely exploited to decorate the imperial pieces with court and hunting scenes and figures of fantastic animals. The lion's share of Sasanian metalwork is in Russia, having from an early period been traded up the great rivers for slaves and furs, but the Museum possesses some fine examples. A parcel-gilt silver dish (Plate 1) shows a carved and engraved figure of the "senmurv"– a strange mixture of lion, peacock, and dog. The figure and border are left silver, the background is thickly gilded. This dish may date from the 7th century or may be post-Sasanian, for in metalwork, as in the other arts, Sasanian traditions were strong and continued largely unmodified on the confines of Persia, especially in the mountainous area south of the Caspian Sea, where local Persian dynasties held out for a hundred years after the Arab conquest. A parcel-gilt dish[1] in the Hermitage with a mounted bowman shooting a lion bears the name of Sharwen the Masmoghan, a dynasty which ruled Damavand, south of the Caspian Sea, until 758/9. A second piece[2] in the Hermitage, with a representation of the goddess Anahit seated on a griffin and playing a flute, has an inscription which reads: "Property

---

[1] J. ORBELI: "Sasanian and Early Islamic Metalwork", *A Survey of Persian Art*, Ed. A. U. Pope, London and New York, 1939, Vol. IV, Pl. 217.   [2] J. ORBELI: op. cit., Vol. IV, Pl. 225a.

of Dadhburzmihr, son of Farrukhan Gilgilan, Spahbedh of Khurasan". This also was made in North Persia in the first half of the 8th century.

The power of the Caliphate, at its height in the East in the second half of the 8th century, declined rapidly in the 9th century. By the 10th century Persia and Mesopotamia were divided between native Persian dynasties, of which the most powerful were the Buwayhids (932–1055) in South Persia and Mesopotamia, and the Samanids (819–1004), who ruled East Persia and Transoxiana. Little of the metalwork of this period has survived. A gold jug[3] in the Kevorkian Collection is decorated in low relief with rams and winged creatures within stiff scrollwork. A Kufic inscription gives the name of Abu Mansur Bakhtiyar (died 978), a member of the Buwayhid dynasty, which played the part of "mayors of the palace" to the now enfeebled caliphs at Baghdad. A second gold jug,[4] with "Sasanian" peacocks in medallions, bears an inscription containing the name of Samsam al-dawla, a Buwayhid who reigned from 985 to 998. There are two silver jugs[5] in the Hermitage, which may be representative of the metalwork of the Samanids, the richness of whose material culture has been revealed by excavations at Afrasiyab (Old Samarkand) and Nishapur in Khurasan. One is carved in low relief with full and half palmettes enclosing birds embossed in the round, a feature which assumed considerable importance in later Persian work. There is also a silver treasure[6] in the Gulistan Museum, Teheran, of thirteen pieces, seven of which bear the name of Amir Abu'l 'Abbas Walkin ibn Harun, who may be a Daylamite prince who lived in Azerbaijan alongside the Buwayhids about 957. The treasure consists of bottles, bowls, vases and ewers of good simple shape, decorated with engraved and nielloed inscriptions.

In the 11th century the Persian dynasties were swept away by the Seljuk Turks, a nomad people from the Kirghiz Steppe. In 1055 Tughril Beg, the first of the Great Seljuks, entered Baghdad and was officially proclaimed Sultan by the caliph. Under the three Great Seljuks, Tughril Beg (1037–1063), Alp Arslan (1063–1072) and Malik Shah (1072–1092) – the two latter assisted by the great Persian minister, Nizam al Mulk, whose policy it was to settle and Persianize the nomad Turks, and to make of their chief a *King of Kings* in the Sasanian manner – the whole of the Near East, except Egypt, was conquered. In the early 12th century Asia Minor, Syria, and Mesopotamia fell away into the hands of small feudal dynasties, the representatives of which were called Atabegs, originally manumitted slaves who became regents (atabegs) and finally usurped the power of their charges. Persia soon followed suit, the last worthy representative of the Seljuk line being Sultan Sinjar, who died in 1157 defending East Persia against tribes from across the Oxus. Towards the end of the 12th century the Shahs of Khwarizm (Khiva on the lower Oxus) conquered most of East Persia. The arrival of the Mongols put a speedy end to their ambitions.

The Seljuk period, one of the greatest in Persian art, has left behind few examples of work in precious metal. Little of the mass of material – mostly in Russia – published

---

[3] R. HARARI: "Metalwork after the Early Islamic Period", *A Survey of Persian Art*, Ed. A. U. Pope London and New York, 1939, Vol. VI, Pl. 1343.    [4] G. WIET: *Soieries Persanes*. Mémoires de l'Institut d'Égypte. T. 52. Cairo 1947. Pl. XX. The Buwayhid jugs are not universally accepted as genuine.    [5] Y. I. SMIRNOV: Ed. *Oriental Silver (Argenterie orientale)*, (Imperial Archæological Commission), St. Petersburg, 1909, Pls. LXXI–LXXII.    [6] R. HARARI: op. cit., Vol. VI, Pls. 1345–6.

by Smirnov[7] can be confidently placed or dated, though no doubt much of it was made
in Central Asia, the Caucasus region and South Russia, under the inspiration, more or
less direct, of Persian work. Over the well-known silver salver[8] in the Boston Museum
of Fine Arts, which is dated A.H. 457/1066 A.D. and, according to the inscription, was
made by an artist of Kashan and given by a queen to Alp Arslan, opinion is divided – its
indifferent quality being the only point of general agreement. A silver candlestick,[9]
recently acquired by the Boston Museum, bears the name of Sultan Sinjar (1118–57)
and, according to the inscription, was made in A.H. 523/1137 A.D. Its authenticity,
however, will probably not go unquestioned. A series of silver vases and bottles
in the Hermitage[10] with engraved and nielloed decoration and inscriptions, gives
a good idea of 12th and 13th century work. It includes a tray which bears the name of
Khwarizm Shah Abu (ibn?) Ibrahim (end of the 12th century?). The Harari Treasure,
which is said to come from Rayy, includes some 12th century pieces.[11] Two of the
finest 12th to 13th century pieces are a jug and bowl,[12] in the Staatliche Museen, Berlin.
The jug shows cast and engraved decoration of addorsed birds and friezes of running
animals against a background of arabesques. The bowl has a fine nielloed inscription
and arabesque medallions, and in the centre a repoussé figure of a musician. Of this
period the only examples in precious metal in the Museum are a gold bowl (Plate 4b
and c) and a silver amulet case and set of ornaments, said to have been found at Nihavand in West Persia. The cup, with its engraved ducks, circles of arabesques and Kufic
inscription, which compares wine to a sun in a garment of red Chinese silk, is a charming
object. The amulet-case has filigree ornament against a background of niello; on some
of the ornaments the niello is applied in the design in discs in the manner of incrustation.
This use of niello was popular among the nomads on the borders of North-east Persia,
and perhaps the ornaments originally came from that area.

Alongside the plate in precious metals was produced much work in bronze, which was
cast and engraved and, in more elaborate pieces, pierced with openwork. Most of this
work is quite humble, but the shapes are sturdy and the engraving vigorous. Only
occasionally, as on the 10th–11th century bowl with the engraved figure of a horseman
formerly in the Martin Collection,[13] did the craftsman feel justified in signing his work.
The objects produced include mirrors, mortars, incense-burners, bottles, penboxes, buckets
and ewers. A well-known type of mirror (Plate 5a) was probably common all over the
Islamic world, specimens having been found in Mesopotamia and Egypt, as well as in
Persia. The ewers are still of Sasanian type, with pear-shaped body and handle topped
with palmette or pomegranate. The bulk of this material is said to have been found in
North-east and East Persia, in Sistan and Khurasan – the American Expedition found
a fine ewer at Nishapur[14] – though some pieces have also been found in Central and
West Persia, at Rayy, Hamadan, and Nihavand. We know, from literary sources, that

[7] Y. I. SMIRNOV: op. cit.    [8] R. HARARI: op. cit., Vol. VI, Pls. 1347–8.    [9] *Bulletin of the Museum
of Fine Arts, Boston*, February 1949, Vol. XLVII. No. 267.    [10] Y. I. SMIRNOV: op. cit., Pls. LXXXII–
LXXXIII.    [11] R. HARARI: op. cit., Vol. VI, Pls. 1349–1352.    [12] R. HARARI: op. cit., Vol. VI,
Pl. 1353a and b.    [13] G. WIET: *L'Exposition persane de* 1931, (Publications du Musée Arabe du
Caire), Cairo, 1933, Pl. IV. top.    [14] M. S. DIMAND: "A Review of Sasanian and Islamic Metal-
work in A Survey of Persian Art" *Ars Islamica*, Vol. VIII. 1941, Fig. 20.

Khurasan and Sistan had a developed metal industry at this period. Cast and incised bronzes in this style continued to be made alongside the more sumptuous inlaid pieces into the 14th century and later. An incense burner[15] in theMoser Collection, Historisches Museum, Berne, is signed by Ustad Husayn of Isfahan and dated A.H. 725/1325 A.D. The decoration of these pieces consists mainly of panels and friezes of running animals against arabesque backgrounds, medallions of birds, sphinxes and griffins, and benedictory inscriptions in Kufic and Naskhi. This class is not well represented in the Museum's collection, and may be seen to better advantage at the Victoria and Albert Museum. A plate (Plate 2a) has carved decoration similar to that on 10th to 11th century "sgraffiato" pottery from North Persia. A fine early mortar (Plate 2b) has the popular "drop" ornament. The bronze stand (Plate 3) has a good profile. Stands of this sort are often elaborately decorated with openwork.

The origins of inlaid metalwork in the Near East are obscure. Copper inlay was probably used as early as the Sasanian period. A bronze ewer,[16] formerly in the Brummer Collection and now in the Metropolitan Museum, New York, with pear-shaped body and a superb lion-handle, is decorated with stylized flowers, in the calyxes of which are cut circular cells, which were certainly filled with an inlay, perhaps copper. A small group of post-Sasanian ewers[17] are inlaid with copper. The finest, in the Hermitage, is decorated with two peacocks facing a palmette tree. The eyes and comb of the peacocks, the eyes in their tails, collars around their necks and leaves on the tree are deeply inlaid with circular and rectangular pieces of copper. This technique, however, seems to have less in common with the methods used by the later schools of copper, silver, and gold inlay than it has with the earlier cold incrustation of turquoise or coloured glass common in Persia and the Steppes.

The 12th century saw the beginning of a technique of inlaying bronze, and later brass, with copper and silver, which was to prove the real glory of Islamic metalwork. Priority in this technique seems to lie with East Persia, especially with the province of Khurasan. The earliest surviving dated piece is a bronze pen-box in the Hermitage.[18] It is decorated with silver inlaid Arabic and Persian inscriptions enhanced with red copper, and is signed by Umar, the son of al-Fazl, and dated A.H. 542/1148 A.D. The inlaid decoration is supplemented by small engraved figures of birds and foliage, as is customary on the early pieces. The exact provenance of the pen-box is not given in the inscriptions, but it is said to have been found in Central Asia and probably derives from East Persia. It is not yet possible to bridge the gap of some three centuries between the penbox and the group of post-Sasanian ewers. This is all the more surprising as gold and silver inlay had been used in China since before the Han dynasty (202 B.C.–220 A.D.), and copper and silver on bronze images in North India for some centuries.

<hr>

[15] R. HARARI: op. cit., Vol. VI, Pl. 1283c.    [16] A. U. POPE: *Masterpieces of Persian Art*, New York, 1945, Pl. 39.    [17] J. ORBELI and C. TREVER: *Orfévrerie sasanide: objets en or, argent et bronze*, Moscow and Leningrad, 1935, Pls. 72, 73, and 74. F. SARRE and F. R. MARTIN: *Die Ausstellung von Meisterwerken muhammedanischer Kunst in München*, 1910. Munich, 1912, Taf. 130. The ewer in Cairo, associated with the last Umayyad Marwan II also had some sort of inlay; cf. F. SARRE: "Die Bronzekanne des Kalifen Marwan II im Arabischen Museum in Kairo", *Ars Islamica*, Vol. I, 1934.    [18] L. GIUZALIAN: *Pamiatniki Epokhi Rustaveli*, Leningrad 1938, pp. 217–226.

viii

The most important example of 12th century metalwork is a small bronze bucket[19] in the Hermitage, formerly in the Bobrinski Collection. According to the inscriptions it was made at Herat, in Khurasan, by the caster Muhammad ibn 'Abd al Wahid and the in-layer Mas'ud ibn Ahmad in A.H. 559/1163 A.D., for a merchant of Zanjan in North-west Persia. It thus illustrates not only how elaborately the craftsmen were organized in their guilds, but also the statement of the 13th century geographer, Kazwini, that metal vessels inlaid with silver were made in Herat and exported. The elaborate copper and silver inlaid decoration of the bucket is disposed in five bands, two with festive, court, and hunting scenes, and three with Kufic and Naskhi inscriptions, the verticals of the letters ending in human and animal heads and bodies. This last feature, often fantasti-cally contrived, is common on Persian metalwork.

The technique of inlaying was an elaborate one. Narrow lines of inlay, as in arabesques, were inserted in an undercut groove and burnished home or, in skimpier work, burnished on to a line of stippled dots. For larger parts of the design slightly sunken beds of the necessary shape were made in the bronze. The sides were under-cut and the plates of the metal to be inlaid were burnished into position. Details had then to be chased on the silver inlay. The 13th century piece (Plate 23) gives a good idea of the technique. Engraved arabesques, the interspaces filled with a black mastic, provided a delicate background to the inlay: the whole giving a colour scheme of dark bronze or yellow brass, gold, silver or red copper inlay and black mastic. Few pieces have retained their original appearance, but the pen-box (Plate 32) is in almost perfect condition.

Several other 12th century pieces by Khurasani craftsmen are known. They include another bucket in a private collection in Leningrad[20] and an inkwell [21] in the Walters Art Gallery, signed by Heratis. A bottle[22] in the Staatliche Museen, Berlin, and an inkwell[23] in the Metropolitan Museum, New York, are both signed by 'Abd al-Razzak of Nishapur. A fine inkwell of this type, decorated with engraved animals, silver inscriptions and margins of red copper, is in the Museum (Plate 5b).

Also from Herat comes the body of a ewer in the Tiflis Museum.[24] It was inlaid with copper and silver in A.H. 577/1181 A.D. at Herat by Mahmud ibn Muhammad of Herat, who seems to have composed the complacent verses extolling its quality. Its fluted body is covered with arabesques and ribbons, ending in human, bird, and animal heads, and on the shoulder are depicted the twelve signs of the Zodiac. A ewer of this shape, in the Museum,[25] also has embossed birds and lions on the shoulders and neck, and a crouching lion over the uptilted spout. It is lavishly inlaid with silver and copper and was certainly made before the end of the 12th century. Of similar type, but with a

---

[19] R. HARARI: op. cit., Vol. VI, Pl. 1308.  [20] V. KRATCHKOVSKAYA: "Calligraphy. C. Naskhi Inscriptions", *A Survey of Persian Art*, ed. A. U. Pope, London and New York, 1939. Vol. II, p. 1774, Note 3.  [21] R. ETTINGHAUSEN: "The Bobrinski Kettle, Patron and Style of an Islamic Bronze", *Gazette des Beaux Arts*, 1943, Vol. XXIV, Fig. 4.  [22] R. HARARI: op. cit., Vol. VI, Pl. 1311 D.  [23] *Bulletin of the Metropolitan Museum of New York*, Vol. VII. No. 5. Jan., 1949, p. 139.  [24] L. GIUZALIAN: op. cit., pp. 227–236. The best illustration of this important piece is to be found in G. RADDE: *Die Sammlungen des Kaukasischen Museums* (Museum Caucasicum), Tiflis, 1902, Bd. V, Taf. XV.  [25] R. HARARI: op. cit., Vol. VI, Pl. 1326. (The foot is a later addition, the stopper does not belong.)

twelve-sided body, is the magnificent ewer on Plates 6 and 7. This ewer, which is of brass, which began to supplant bronze as the body material in the early 13th century, is one of the finest known. The signs of the Zodiac and the elaborate scrollwork are all inlaid with silver. Copper is used merely for the eyes of the embossed birds. It may be dated in the early 13th century. This type of ewer, commonly imitated in pottery, and a group of candlesticks[26] with similar decoration, may all be attributed on the evidence of the Tiflis piece to East and Central Persia.

Two varieties of "animated" inscription may be seen on the body of the ewer (Plate 7). An even more elaborate example may be seen on the brass vase (Plate 8). Here monkeys, birds and snakes are entangled in the human-headed shafts of the letters.

The bronze flask and brass bucket (Plates 9 and 10) also date from about 1200. The flask was obtained in the Punjab, but was probably made in East Persia, for the Ghurid dynasty held Herat, Afghanistan and North India at this period. The rosette of seven dots is a common feature. The bucket, the base of which is also decorated – the sure sign of a fine piece was perhaps made in Transoxiana, though it obviously derives from Persian models.

In 1220–1 Genghis Khan invaded Transoxiana and Khurasan. Bukhara, Samarkand, Balkh, Merv, Nishapur and Herat, all centres of the metal industry, were sacked. Craftsmen were usually spared in the general massacre and often carried off to Kara-korum and other Mongol centres, where no doubt they worked in the company of their fellow artisans of the Far East. The bronze mortar (Plate 11) is an interesting example of such a mixture of styles. The massive shape, the inscription below the rim, and the seven-dot rosettes point to Persia. The remainder of the decoration and the use of thin lines of silver and copper, deeply set, are Chinese. On the base is a Chinese inscription in seal characters, also inlaid with thin copper wire, which asks the owner to treat the mortar as a precious possession.

Three important dated pieces, made on the eve of the Mongol invasion, should also be mentioned. A silver inlaid bronze aquamanile[27] in the shape of a cow with its young being attacked by a lion, in the Academy of Sciences, Kiev, was made by 'Ali ibn Muhammad in A.H. 603/1206 A.D. It has been suggested that this fine, but archaistic, bronze, was made in North-west Persia or the Caucasus region. A pen-box,[28] in the Freer Gallery in Washington, was made by one, Shadhi, in A.H. 607/1210 A.D., for the Grand Vizier of Khurasan, whose headquarters were at Merv. The "animated" inscription is similar to those on the Museum's ewer and vase (Plates 6, 7 and 8). Finally, an astrolabe,[29] in the Old Ashmolean, Oxford, is decorated round its rim with silver inlaid signs of the Zodiac. It is dated A.H. 618/1221–2 A.D. by the artist who proudly calls himself "the needlemaker of Isfahan". Isfahan had been famous for these instruments for centuries, the earliest dated specimen known[30] (A.H. 374/984–5 A.D.) also having been made there.

---

[26] R. HARARI: op. cit., Vol. VI, Pl. 1321. These candlesticks frequently have free standing birds around the shoulder, in addition to the embossed decoration. [27] *Mémoires IIIe Congrès International d'Art et d'Archéologie Iraniens, Leningrad, Septembre,* 1935, Moscow-Leningrad, 1939, Pls. XXIV–XXV. [28] E. HERZFELD: "A Bronze Pen-case", *Ars Islamica,* Vol. III, 1936. [29] R. HARARI: op. cit., Vol. VI, Pls. 1312 D. and E and 1398. [30] R. HARARI: op. cit., Vol. VI, Pl. 1397 A. and B.

Little has remained of what must once have been a flourishing metalwork industry in Mesopotamia during the 12th century and earlier. In the watershed of the Tigris and Euphrates there are rich copper mines at Arghana, between Kharput and Diarbakr, which were worked from an early period. Both the caliphs in their domain around Baghdad, and the numerous small dynasties in the independent cities of North Mesopotamia, must have used plate of precious metal, but none which can with certainty be ascribed to this area has survived. Mirrors of the type of Plate 5a were no doubt made in Mesopotamia. Two mirrors[31] in the Harari Collection, dated A.H. 548/1153 A.D. and A.H. 675/1276 A.D., and decorated with representations of the planets, signs of the Zodiac, and running animals, are probably of North Mesopotamian origin. A third mirror[32] in the Wallerstein Collection, bears the name of Urtuq Shah, the Urtukid ruler of Kharput in the middle of the 13th century. Interesting series of coins were struck by many cities during the late 12th and 13th centuries with figural representations, some of which hark back to Antiochid, Roman, and Sasanian types. Undoubtedly, the finest piece of metalwork attributable to Mesopotamia in the 12th century is the bronze cloisonné-enamelled plate[33] in the Ferdinandeum at Innsbruck. It is decorated in polychrome enamels with a throned figure surrounded by dancers, palmettes, and medallions of bird, animal, and figure subjects. It was made for the Urtukid Rukn al Dawla Dawud (1108–45), ruler of Kayfa and Amida in North Mesopotamia. This magnificent plate is, unfortunately, unique, though there is good reason to believe that the technique of cloisonné-enamel was originally a Persian invention.

There is no direct evidence of inlaid metalwork having been made in Mesopotamia before the beginning of the 13th century, when a flourishing industry suddenly appears. The most important centre of production seems to have been the town of Mosul, on the right bank of the Upper Tigris opposite the ancient Nineveh. Mosul was ruled from 1127 to 1233 by the Seljuk Atabegs of the Zangid dynasty, the founder of which was the famous anti-crusader, 'Imad al-din (1127–46), and from 1233 to 1259 by Badr al-din Lulu, the vizier of the last of the Zangids. There are some twenty-five pieces,[34] signed by Mosul artists, the earliest of which is a small box[35] in the Benaki Museum, Athens. It is dated A.H. 617/1220 A.D. and was made by Isma 'il ibn Ward of Mosul, the pupil of Ibrahim ibn Mawlid of Mosul. Unfortunately, no works of the last-named master have survived. The box is already an assured piece of craftsmanship, making full use of the new "Mosul" ornament and its disposition. The most important single piece signed by a Mosul artist is, without doubt, the ewer (Plate 12). An inscription around the neck states that it was made by Shuja' ibn Man'a of Mosul, in Mosul in A.H. 629/1232 A.D. A comparison of this superb piece with the roughly contemporary Persian ewer (Plates 6 and 7) will show how distinct the two styles were, in spite of some general similarities,

---

[31] R. HARARI: op. cit., Vol. VI, Pl. 1301 A. and B.    [32] F. SARRE and F. R. MARTIN: op. cit., Taf. 140.    [33] F. SARRE and F. R. MARTIN: op. cit., Taf. 159.    [34] A list, to which should be added the ewer in the Walters Art Gallery signed by Yunus ibn Yusuf of Mosul and dated A.H. 644/1246 A.D., is to be found in E. KÜHNEL: Zwei Mosulbronzen und ihr Meister, *Jahrbuch der preussischen Kunstsammlungen*, Band 60, 1939, pp. 9–11.    [35] *Exposition d'Art Musulman, Les Amis de l'Art, Alexandrie, mars*, 1925, Pl. 10, top.

and that if the Mosul craftsman was debtor to the Persian, he had borrowed little more than the technique. Both ewers are of brass – Persia was beginning to abandon the use of bronze, and Mosul appears rarely to have used it for inlaid work – and on both the disposition of the main figural motifs is in lobed medallions. Here the similarity ends. Instead of the loose arabesques on the unworked brass background, the Mosul artist preferred, though not exclusively, a complete covering of the vessel with various angular motifs or closely-curling arabesques. The repertory of ornament of the two pieces is obviously quite distinct. It is interesting to compare the "animated" inscriptions: that running round the body of the Mosul ewer, between the rows of inlaid subject medallions, is even more fantastically composed than, and has nothing in common with, the conventions of Persia. Mosul craftsmen, like the Persians, frequently used the twelve signs of the Zodiac as the main figure ornament of their vessels, though they were also very fond of court and genre scenes. The seven planetary signs rarely occur apart from the figure representing the moon, which sits crossed legged holding a crescent around his face. This motif is very common on pieces of Mosul type, appearing also on the Sinjar Gate of Mosul and on its coins. It remains to add that on the Mosul ewer generous use of bands of red copper is made in the figure scenes, the background to which is provided by delicately engraved arabesques in the brass.

A fine early Mosul piece is the writing box (Plates 14 and 15a and b). It also makes clever use of copper in outlining the silver-inlaid figures of signs of the Zodiac. The pearled quatrefoils and circling birds or animals, as on the base of this piece (page XXIV), are very common on early examples.

Not all the pieces signed by Mosul artists were made in that city – indeed it will be seen that the inscriptions on some definitely state that they were made elsewhere – but there is a small group of six pieces which can be assigned to Mosul itself with certainty. The most important piece is the ewer (Plates 12 and 13): of the remainder, four bear the name of Badr al-din Lulu and one the name of a courtier of his. The outstanding Lulu piece is a silver inlaid dish[36] in the State Library of Munich, the centre of which is decorated with circling sphinxes and griffons. A box in the Museum (Plate 18), with circling geese on the lid and typical "Mosul" background to the small figure medallions, also bears this ruler's name. It is interesting to note that the artist has utilized the seven-dot rosette so common in Persia. On a dish in the Victoria and Albert Museum, the centre of which is also decorated with large circling sphinxes, the rest of the field has been left unworked.

An exceptionally fine piece is the astronomical table (Plates 16 and 17), made by Muhammad ibn Khutlukh of Mosul in A.H. 639/1241–2 A.D. Especially noteworthy are the lovely pattern in silver on the back and the gold and silver inscriptions on the front. Gold was now beginning to take the place of copper as a foil to the silver inlay. North Mesopotamia was a noted centre for applied science and astronomy. An astronomical globe in the Museum, with incised figures of the constellations and silver inlaid stars and inscription, was made or designed in A.H. 674/1275 A.D. by the astronomer

[36] F. SARRE and M. VAN BERCHEM: "Das Metallbecken des Atabegs Lulu von Mosul in der Kgl. Bibliotek zu München", *Münchner Jahrbuch der bildenden Kunst*, 1907.

Muhammad ibn Hilal of Mosul.[37] The incense burner (Plate 15c) is also of North Mesopotamia manufacture. It is dated A.H. 641/1243–4 A.D., and around the top runs the
characteristic inscription, "within me is hell fire: without float the sweetest odours".

Few signed Mosul pieces of the second half of the 13th century can be attributed with
certainty to that city, but there is no reason to think that production died out there.
Lulu had had the wit to recognise Mongol suzerainty and his city had, unlike most other
North Mesopotamian cities, not been sacked. His son was less prudent and rebelled: he
was killed by the Mongols and his city plundered in 1261–2. No doubt many craftsmen
were carried off by the Mongols to their capitals in North-west Persia. Mosul was,
however, still an art centre in the early 14th century, and the latest dated pieces are
consistently developed from the early style. The last Mosul artist known to have
signed and dated a piece is 'Ali ibn 'Umar ibn Ibrahim, who made a candlestick,[38] in
the Benaki Museum, Athens, in A.H. 717/1317 A.D.

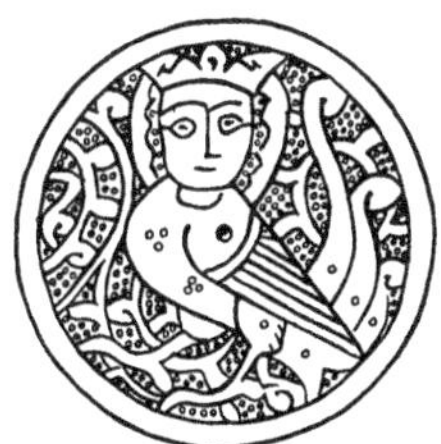

## SYRIA AND EGYPT, 10TH TO 16TH CENTURY

The declining power of the Caliphate in the 9th century enabled Ahmad ibn Tulun,
the son of a Turkish slave, to become virtually independent in Egypt and Syria. The
dynasty he founded was shortlived (868 to 905). It was followed by the Ikhshidids (935
to 969), who were themselves supplanted by the Fatimids (969 to 1171). The Fatimids,
whose earlier capital had been near Tunis, removed the seat of government to Cairo and
thus inaugurated one of the most brilliant periods in Islamic history. Comparatively
little of their material culture, which was an object of wonder to their contemporaries,
has survived. The luxurious gold and silversmith's work, described by Nasir-i-
Khusrau, who made an inspection of the state apartments in 1047, and by the early
15th century historian, Maqrizi, who, from early archives, made an inventory of the
treasures stored in the palaces, is now represented only by pieces of jewellery, exquisitely
wrought in gold wire with turquoise and cloisonné-enamel inlay.[39] Cloisonné-enamel
was without doubt extensively used by the Fatimids – Maqrizi mentions gold plaques
with coloured enamels – but next to nothing has survived. A delightful small medallion,[40] with foliated ornament and an inscription enamelled on gold, was found at

---

[37] *Transactions of the Royal Asiatic Society*, 1830, ii, pp. 371–392.　[38] *Exposition d'Art Musulman,
Les Amis de l'Art, Alexandrie, mars*, 1925, Pl. 13.　[39] The best collections are in the Harari Collection; Arab Museum, Cairo; Benaki Museum, Athens; and Metropolitan Museum, New York.
[40] G. MIGEON: *Manuel d'Art Musulman*, Paris, 1927, II, Fig. 222.

Fostat and is now in the Arab Museum, Cairo. The quality of Fatimid gold and silver-smith's work, like the painting, can best be imagined by comparison with work done in the centres under Fatimid influence. The silver-gilt casket [41] in the Cathedral of Gerona, made for a courtier of al-Hakam II (961–976) to give to the heir-apparent, Hisham, who succeeded his father as Caliph at Cordova, shows how magnificent the Egyptian models must have been.

Cast and engraved bronzes were also made in Egypt and Syria as in Persia. A common type of standing lamp (Plate 4a) is obviously derived from Coptic prototypes. The most important bronzes are, however, a small group of animals, some of which influenced the development of the European aquamanile. The finest is the huge griffin [42] which stands in the Campo Santo at Pisa. This monumental bronze, the body of which is entirely covered with engraved designs, is a remarkable piece of casting. Another fine example is a stag in the Nazionalmuseum at Munich. [43]

In 1171 the Fatimid dynasty was succeeded by the Ayyubid, the founder of which was Salah-al-din (Saladin). Salah-al-din's empire extended from Egypt to the Euphrates, and even the rulers of the North Mesopotamian cities recognized his suzerainty. When he died in 1193, his sons succeeded in the various provinces, but his brother, Sayf-al-din 'Adil (Saphadin) gradually acquired the supreme authority. 'Adil's line continued at Cairo and Damascus, the direct descendants of Saladin being able to hold out only at Aleppo.

The Ayyubid period saw the beginning of inlaid metalwork in Syria and Egypt. The philologist, Ibn Sa'id, travelling in North Mesopotamia about 1250, mentions that the objects of gold and silver inlay, made in quantity at Mosul, were exported to princes. This statement is borne out by surviving pieces. A ewer [44] in the Kevorkian Collection, dated A.H. 624/1227 A.D., was made by Qasim ibn 'Ali, the servant of Ibrahim ibn Mawaliya of Mosul, for the private secretary of Malik al-'Aziz, who is probably 'Aziz Ghiyath al-din Muhammad (1216–36), the Ayyubid ruler of Aleppo. A basin in the Louvre [45] was made by Ahmad ibn 'Umar al-Daki of Mosul for 'Adil Abu Bakr, the Ayyubid ruler of Cairo and Damascus (1238–40). Both ewer and basin are in pure Mosul style. It is impossible to say with certainty if these pieces and various others un-signed but made for Ayyubid rulers, were ordered in Mosul or made in Syria or Egypt. Up to 1245 Lulu had been on good terms with the Ayyubids and had been closely asso-ciated with Ashraf Musa, who ruled the greater part of Mesopotamia and Damascus (1210–37). Lulu's subservience to the Mongols interrupted friendly relations from 1245 to 1259, and it is possible that during this period independent workshops were started at Damascus and perhaps Aleppo. In any case, in the second half of the 13th century Mosul had begun to export not only her products but also her craftsmen. In A.H. 657/1259 A.D., Husayn ibn Muhammad of Mosul made a ewer [46] in Damascus for Nasir Salah-al-din Yusuf, Ayyubid of Aleppo and Damascus (1236–60). The Museum possesses several pieces probably made in Syria at this time. The handwarmer (Plate 22) was made

[41] G. MIGEON: op. cit., II, Fig. 220.　[42] G. MIGEON: op. cit., I, Fig. 182.　[43] F. SARRE and F. R. MARTIN: op. cit., Taf. 155.　[44] E. KÜHNEL: op. cit., Abb. 9　[45] G. MIGEON: *L'Orient Musulman*, (Musée du Louvre. Documents d'Art), Paris, 1922, Pl. 29.　[46] G. MIGEON: op. cit., Pl. 31. No. 89.

for Badr al-din Baysari, whose blazon, the double-headed eagle, appears several times on the piece in openwork. Baysari had been one of the mamluks (white slaves) of the last reigning Ayyubid. In 1250 the Mamluks seized power from their masters and there followed a succession of slave kings, divided into two dynasties, the Bahri (of the River) and the Burji (of the Fort) who ruled Egypt and Syria down to the beginning of the 16th century. Baysari had a colourful career. He rose to the rank of a Commander of a Thousand, and was imprisoned three times; and it was in prison that he died in 1298-9. He had, in 1252, as a young man, ordered a basin, now in the Musée des Arts Décoratifs in Paris, from Dawud ibn Salama of Mosul. His handwarmer is also in Mosul style and may be dated between 1264 and 1279. A salver, a detail from which is illustrated (Plate 23), may also have been made for him and certainly dates from the same period. Most of the silver has been lost, thus enabling one to see how the inlay was effected. The candlestick (Plate 24) was also probably made in Syria during the last decades of the century.

An interesting series of vessels, some of which were probably made in Syria, are decorated with Christian subjects and figures. The Ayyubids were often on friendly terms with the Christian kingdoms of Syria, and no doubt the more sumptuous of these pieces were made as gifts for them. A very fine piece is the silver inlaid basin[47] in the collection of the Duke of Arenberg, which contains five medallions with representations of the Annunciation, Mary and the Child, the Raising of Lazarus, the Entry into Jerusalem and the Last Supper. It is inscribed with the name of Salih Najm al-din Ayyub (Cairo: 1240–9; Damascus: 1240 and 1245–9). Another famous piece, signed by Dawud ibn Salama of Mosul in A.H. 646/1248 A.D., is a candlestick[48] in the Musée des Arts Décoratifs, Paris, also decorated with scenes from the life of Christ, and with rows of saints. A third piece,[49] a bronze pilgrim bottle, formerly in the Eumorfopoulos Collection and now in the Freer Gallery, Washington, is similarly decorated. Some of the warriors depicted are shooting with the European crossbow and are presumably meant to represent Crusaders. The incense-burner (Plate 21) belongs to this group. The deacon (Plate 21b) is an especially impressive figure.

Syria did not settle down to enjoy undisturbed the prosperity of Egypt under the early Mamluks until the beginning of the 14th century: Aleppo having been sacked by the Mongols in 1260, 1280, and 1299, and Damascus in 1260 and 1300. It was probably soon after 1300 that there was produced the most splendid piece of inlaid metalwork[50] that has survived, the so-called Baptistère de St. Louis in the Louvre, the work of the master, Muhammad ibn al-Zayn. The inlay on this piece, a miracle of patient craftsmanship, does not obscure the grandeur of the general design. A gold and silver inlaid mirror[51] in the Topkapu Serai Museum, Istanbul, is of the same quality. These pieces, though derived from the 13th century Mosul style, show an even greater virtuosity in the elaborate chasing of details on the silver. The writing box (Plate 25) and the incense-burner (Plate 26a) are good examples of the first half of the 14th century.

[47] F. SARRE and F. R. MARTIN: op. cit., Taf. 146.  [48] F. SARRE and F. R. MARTIN: op. cit., Taf. 147.  [49] M. S. DIMAND: "A silver inlaid Bronze Canteen with Christian subjects in the Eumorfopoulos Collection", *Ars Islamica*. Vol. I, 1934.  [50] R. HARARI: op. cit., Vol. VI, Pl. 1339.  [51] M. AGA OGLU: "Ein Prachtspiegel im Topkapu Serayi Museum", *Pantheon II*, 1930.

XV

The Syrian school continued to flourish until the end of the 14th century. Simono Sigoli,[52] an Italian traveller who visited Damascus between 1384 and 1385, mentions the large numbers of brass basins and ewers made there and inlaid with figures, foliage and other delicate designs in silver. It was the craftsmen responsible for these that Timur is said to have taken off to Samarkand after the sack of Damascus in 1401. Nevertheless, it is difficult to attribute any pieces to the second half of the 14th century. Either the same style continued to the end or else it became assimilated to that of Cairo.

The earliest piece of inlaid metalwork, the inscription on which states explicitly that it was made in Cairo, is an astrolabe (Plates 19 and 20). It was made by 'Abd al Karim, of Cairo, the astrolabist and follower of Malik Ashraf, Malik Mu'izz and Shihab (al-din), in the year A.H. 633/1236 A.D. Malik Ashraf is probably the Ayyubid who ruled in Mesopotamia (1210–30) and Damascus (1228–37). The identity of the other two patrons is doubtful.[53] The body of this magnificent instrument, probably the finest known, is inlaid front and back with silver: on the figures and foliage of the ankabut copper is lavishly used. Apart from vessels made in Mosul style, and in some cases by Mosul artists, for the Ayyubids of Cairo, no piece can be definitely attributed to that city until the seventies of the century. 'Ali ibn Husayn ibn Muhammad of Mosul, the son of the artist who signed the ewer made in Damascus in 1259, himself made a splendid ewer[54] in A.H. 674/1275 A.D. in Cairo for Muzaffar Yusuf (? 1249–95), a Rasulid sultan of the Yemen. The Rasulids (1229–1454) seem to have ordered most of their fine plate from Cairo. From now on until the early 14th century, there is a series of excellent pieces signed by Mosul artists in Cairo, all representing an extension of the Mosul style with a growing predilection for large inscriptions as the main part of the design.

In the early 14th century new decorative motifs appear, derived apparently from Chinese textiles and porcelain. They include formally rendered flower and leaf borders and the Chinese lotus, which appears in beautifully varied forms (Plate 28). The lotus motif had been used slightly earlier in Persia, where the new repertoire of ornament had also been adopted. A good example of the early 14th century, with typical radiating inscription on the lid, borders of leaves and medallions of flying birds, is the box (Plate 26b). A fine early piece in the fully-developed new style is the writing box (Plate 27). Many excellent pieces bear the name or titles of the Mamluk Sultan Nasir al-din Muhammad ibn Kalaun (1293, 1298–1308 and 1309–40) or his courtiers. The most important is a wonderful Kursi (table)[55] in the Arab Museum, Cairo, with openwork decoration and silver and gold inlay, which is signed by the master, Muhammad ibn Sunqur of Baghdad, and dated A.H. 728/1327 A.D. The Museum possesses several pieces with Nasir Muhammad's name or titles, conspicuous among

---

[52] *Viaggio al Monte Sinai*, Parma, 1843, pp. 61 ff. Quoted by M. AGA OGLU: "About a type of Islamic Incense Burner", *Art Bulletin*, March, 1945, Vol. XXVII, No. I.　[53] For another interpretation, see VAN BERCHEM: *Notes d'archéologie arabe*, IIIe article, 1904, p. 32, Note 2. A second astrolabe, made by 'Abd al Karim (?), servant of Malik Ashraf, in A.H. 625/1227–8 A.D., and inlaid sparingly with silver and gold, is in the Old Ashmolean. See A. GUNTHER: *Astrolabes of the World*, Oxford, 1932, Vol. I, p. 233, and Pls. LIII and LIV.　[54] In the Musée des Arts Décoratifs, Paris. G. MIGEON: *Manuel d'Art Musulman*, Paris, 1927, II, Fig. 261.　[55] G. WIET: *Objets en cuivre* (Catalogue général du Musée Arabe du Caire), Cairo, 1932, Pls. I–II.

which are a large basin (Plate 28) and a bowl.[56] The base of a very fine ewer, in the Museum (Plate 29b), shows how assured and intricate the gold and silver inlay was. A large silver-inlaid circular tray in the Museum in the same style, bears the name of the Sultan Sha'ban (1345–46). There was no decline in quality during the second half of the 14th century.

Soon after 1400 there was a falling off both in quality and quantity. Makrizi, writing about 1420, says that in his time the demand for inlaid metalwork had seriously declined, and that only a small number of craftsmen survived. Probably Chinese blue-and-white porcelain, now flooding the markets of the Near East, was beginning to supplant the more expensive inlaid metalwork. But good work in cut iron was still made, and occasionally one finds a fine piece of inlaid metalwork. A basin,[57] in Istanbul, decorated in gold and silver, with entrelacs and arabesques, bears the name of the Sultan Kait-Bey (1468–96). But the best work was done by the armsmiths. Fine shape and clean decoration make the parcel-gilt, inlaid steel helmet (Plate 30) an impressive object. The technique of inlay is different from that on the earlier pieces. Here the silver, used very thin, is burnished direct on to the surface to be inlaid, which has previously been stippled with a tool. When secure the inlay was exposed to heat until it sweated. Unpretentious engraved vessels (Plate 31) of fair quality were made during the 16th century under Ottoman rule.

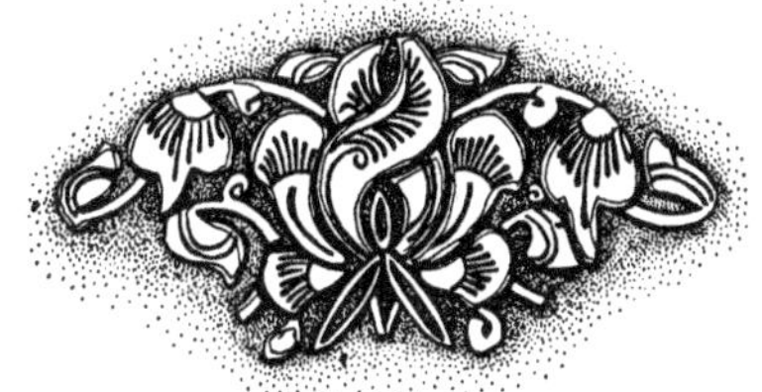

## PERSIA, 13TH TO 18TH CENTURY

Apart from a destructive raid across North Persia, the Mongol invasion of 1220–1 affected Transoxiana and Khurasan only. West Persia enjoyed a brief respite, but all went down before the full-scale invasion of 1231. From 1231 to 1256, Mongol control consisted of two independent armies: one, based on the rich pastures of North-east Azerbaijan, subjected and terrorized North Mesopotamia and Asia Minor, the other, in Khurasan, bled the country for tribute. In 1256, the position was regularised. Hulagu, the younger brother of the Great Khan, arrived with orders to extend Mongol rule to the borders of Egypt. He captured Baghdad and put an end to the Caliphate in 1258. He made a permanent settlement of his conquests and founded the dynasty of the Ilkhans, which, with capitals at Maragha, Tabriz and Sultaniya in North-west Persia, ruled until 1335.

<hr>

[56] S. LANE-POOLE: *The Art of the Saracens in Egypt*, London, 1886, Fig. 87.   [57] F. SARRE and F. R. MARTIN: op. cit., Taf. 158.

Khurasan seems not to have fully revived until the late 14th century, but metalwork of good quality was probably still made in the second half of the 13th century. A silver inlaid candlestick[58] in the Teheran Museum may date from the middle of the century: it represents a modification of the earlier style. A series of candlesticks, whose body has a plain, concave profile and many Persian decorative elements, continued to be made into the 14th century, though it is difficult to say whether poor quality indicates later date or a provincial workshop.

The Persian and Mesopotamian styles, which were clearly separate at the beginning of the 13th century, began to mingle, for not only had Persian artists fled westwards before the Mongols, but the Mongols themselves from their commanding position in Azerbaijan were able to call on artists from throughout their dominions. The Ilkhan Uljaitu (1304–16), for example, ordered his magnificent illuminated Kurans from Mosul, Baghdad, and Hamadan. A ewer in the Victoria and Albert Museum[59] of Persian shape, has the seated man with the new moon as the main decoration of the body. It probably dates from the second half of the 13th century. Again, a ewer [60] of Mosul shape, in the Louvre, has around its shoulder the rather incongruous decoration of freestanding birds in the Persian manner. This ewer is dated A.H. 709/1309 A.D. The difficulty is further illustrated by a find at Hamadan[61] of a number of brass vessels inlaid with silver. Though found in Persia there is little to distinguish these pieces, two of which are signed by a Mosul artist, from Mosul works of the second half of the 13th century.

A difficult piece to place is the pen-box (Plates 32 and 33), inlaid with gold, silver, and black mastic and signed by Mahmud ibn Sunqur in A.H. 680/1281 A.D. This piece is of superb quality, and in addition to the tiny representations of the planets and signs of the Zodiac, and a battle scene on its base, makes use of both Persian and Mesopotamian decorative motifs. It has been asked whether Mahmud was the senior brother of Muhammad ibn Sunqur of Baghdad, who signed the Kursi table, dated A.H. 728/1328 A.D., already mentioned. It may be so, especially as certain decorative elements on the pen-box, such as the loose entrelacs, can be paralleled in slightly later Baghdadi Kurans.

Settled government and a return of prosperity towards the end of the 13th century, revitalized all the arts. In metalwork, as in miniature painting, one finds a conservative Mesopotamian style alongside a new one. Good examples of the former are three bronze balls inlaid with gold and silver, in the Harari Collection, which bear the name of Uljaitu [62] (1304–16), The new style was formed under the influence of Chinese paintings, textiles and the like. Under the "Pax Tartarica" intercourse between the Ilkhans and their brethren in China, who had formed the Yuan Dynasty, was easy and frequent. The new motifs included the lotus, which we have already seen on Mamluk metalwork, and borders of naturalistically-rendered flowers. A fine, large, brass candlestick in the Stora Collection,[63] which is dated A.H. 708/1308 A.D., is the earliest dated

---

[58] R. HARARI: op. cit., Vol. VI, Pl. 1316.  [59] R. HARARI: op. cit., Vol. VI, Pl. 1327. The fluted and twelve-sided ewers continued to be made, in declining quality, into the 14th century. They may have been made even later, since the shape was copied in Ming blue-and-white porcelain of the 15th century.  [60] G. MIGEON: *Orient Musulman* (Musée du Louvre. Documents d'Art), Paris, 1922, Pl. 72.  [61] R. HARARI: op. cit., Vol. VI, Pls. 1331, 1332, 1334, 1341, and 1342a.  [62] R. HARARI: op. cit., Vol. VI, Pl. 1357a.  [63] R. HARARI: op. cit., Vol. VI, Pl. 1355.

example of this new style. The distribution of the silver-inlaid ornament is similar to that on the contemporary Mamluk box on Plate 26b, but the rendering of the peonies and the borders and medallions of flowers reveals its Persian origin. Perhaps the finest example of this style is the magnificent plate with gadrooned rim in the Metropolitan Museum,[64] though the goblet (Plate 34) is worthily representative.

An important piece for the understanding of the development of metalwork during the 14th century is a silver and gold inlaid candlestick in the Harari Collection.[65] It is dated A.H. 761/1360 A.D. and was made by Muhammad ibn Rafi al-din of Shiraz. Shiraz had been seized by the Muzaffarids (1353–93), an Arabo-Persian dynasty, after the break-up of the Ilkhanid Empire. They were great patrons of the arts, and it is probable that the candlestick was made at their capital, which it is known possessed a metal industry. This piece is identical in shape and decoration, except that it has the ubiquitous lotus, with a candlestick in the Museum (Plate 35). The latter has a good Kufic inscription imposed on the larger Thulth. This use of Kufic and Thulth may also be found on a bowl[66] in the Harari Collection, which is wonderfully decorated with elaborate court scenes and floral backgrounds. Another fine bowl[67] in the Walters Art Gallery shows a polo match. The bowl (Plate 36) is a good example of this refined and courtly art. The exaggeratedly tall aristocratic figures with their conical hats are usually compared with those in the book of poems by Khwaju Kirmani (in the Museum), copied in A.H. 799/1396 A.D. in Baghdad, which was ruled by the Mongol Jalayrid dynasty (1336–1411), which had succeeded the Ilkhans in Mesopotamia and North-west Persia.

Also to be dated in the 14th century, though in a somewhat drier style, is a series of caskets and domed boxes, of which the Museum possesses good examples (Plate 37). They are lavishly inlaid with gold and silver, and some of the domed boxes[68] achieve great dignity of shape. A large casket in the Victoria and Albert Museum is the finest of the group.[69]

The end of the 14th century saw the whole of the Near East, less Egypt, overrun by Timur. From the sacked cities, Isfahan (1387), Shiraz (1393), Baghdad (1394 and 1401), and Damascus (1400), this ferocious æsthete carried off artists and men of letters to his capital at Samarkand. In the city of Turkestan, across the Amu Darya, in the Mosque of Ahmad Yasavi, built in 1397 by a Shirazi, are magnificent carved wooden doors, the handles[70] of which, in carved bronze openwork, are signed by 'Izz al din of Isfahan. This artist also signed and dated (A.H. 799/1397 A.D.) a three-foot high silver-inlaid bronze candlestick,[71] in the Hermitage. A huge cauldron,[72] nearly six feet high, in the same mosque in Turkestan, is said to bear the name of an artist of Tabriz. These pieces are sparsely inlaid, and rely for their somewhat barbaric effect on their size and good shapes. They bear little relation to those pieces made in Persia which have survived.

[64] R. HARARI: op. cit., Vol. VI, Pl. 1358. [65] R. HARARI: op. cit., Vol. VI, Pl. 1371. [66] R. HARARI: op. cit., Vol. VI, Pl. 1367a. See also R. ETTINGHAUSEN: "A 14th Century Metal Bowl", *Bulletin of American Institute for Persian Art and Archæology*, June, 1935, Vol. IV, No. I. [67] R. HARARI: op. cit., Vol. VI, Pl. 1367b. [68] R. HARARI: op. cit., Vol. VI, Pls. 1361–2. [69] R. HARARI: op. cit., Vol. VI, Pl. 1359. [70] E. COHN-WIENER: *Turan*, Berlin, 1930, Pl. LX. [71] *IIIe Congrès International d'Art et d'Archéologie Iraniens, Mémoires. Leningrad* 1935. Op. cit., Pl. CXXI. [72] Op. cit., Pls. CXIX and CXXII.

The 15th century is something of a blank in Persian metalwork as in pottery. In Persia as in Egypt the tables of the rich were supplied by Ming blue-and-white porcelain, which, together with its Persian imitations and elaborately wrought vessels in precious metal, are frequently represented in the illuminated manuscripts of the period. The plate has for the most part disappeared, having probably been melted down for bullion, but specimens exist in the Topkapu Sarai Museum of Istanbul as part of the booty of Sultan Selim after his successful expedition against Shah Isma'il in 1514. These pieces, some of which have a silver body parcel-gilt with applied gold plaques and encrusted with precious stones, are fine in their way. They continued to be made with some quality into the 17th century, being sometimes enriched with glassy enamels, the general effect being that of the contemporary Mughal work in India.

With the emergence, in 1502, of a native Persian dynasty, the Safavid, appears much dated material. It consists largely of modestly inlaid and engraved pieces, some of which are of copper, tinned to simulate silver. The shapes are occasionally distinguished, as in the gilt copper ewer (Plate 38a). But the best and most original work was done in cut steel – some of the ornamental plaques in this material are very fine – and by the arms-smiths and instrument makers. The steel armpiece and helmet (Plates 38b and 39), made for Shah 'Abbas the Great (1587–1629) and dated A.H. 1035/1625-6 A.D., are decorated with superbly carved arabesques and gold inlaid inscriptions, which include quotations from the Bustan of Sa'di and from other poets. The astrolabe (Plate 40), made in A.H. 1124/1712 A.D. for Shah Husayn, shows that as late as the 18th century Persian craftsmanship was of a high order.

Shah Husayn was the last of the Safavids. The Afghan invasion, which caused the downfall of his dynasty, impoverished all the arts and brought the long period of original creation in metalwork to a close.

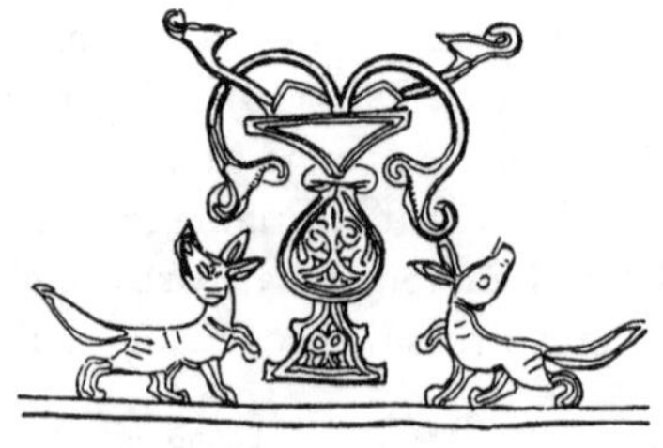

# DESCRIPTION OF PLATES

## REFERENCES

S. LANE-POOLE *The Art of the Saracens in Egypt*, London, 1886. M. VAN BERCHEM "Notes d'archéologie arabe, III: Étude sur les cuivres damasquinés et les verres émaillés", *Journal asiatique*, Series 10, Vol. III (1904), pp. 5–96. G. MIGEON *Manuel d'art musulman: Arts plastiques et industriels*, 2 vols., 2nd edition, Paris, 1927. G. WIET *Objets en cuivre* (Catalogue général du Musée Arabe du Caire), Cairo, 1932. Appendice. Liste chronologique des objets en cuivre à inscriptions historiques, Nos. 1–544.

1    DISH, silver, carved and engraved, parcel-gilt. Sasanian or post-Sasanian. O. M. Dalton: *The Treasure of the Oxus*, London, 1926, p. 66 and pl. XL.
D. 7½ in.: 19 cm. *Given by the National Art Collections Fund*, 1922.

2a    PLATE, bronze, engraved. Persian, X–XI Cent. Unpublished. Acquired in the Yemen.
D. 9 in.: 22·8 cm. *Bought* 1949.

2b    MORTAR, bronze, engraved. Persian, X–XI Cent. Unpublished.
H. 4½ in.: 11·4 cm. *Bought* 1939 (*From Ginsberg Collection*).

3    STAND, bronze, engraved. Persian, XII–XIII Cent. Acquired in Bukhara.
H. 10⅞ in.: 27·6 cm. *Bought* 1905.

4a    LAMP, bronze, engraved. Egyptian, XII–XIII Cent. Unpublished. Acquired in Egypt.
H. 18½ in.: 47 cm. *Bought* 1914.

4b and c    BOWL, gold, engraved. Persian, XI–XII Cent. B. Gray: "A Seljuq Hoard from Persia", *British Museum Quarterly*, Vol. XIII, 1938–9, pp. 73–79.
D. 3 in.: 7·6 cm. *Given by the National Art Collections Fund*, 1938.

5a    MIRROR, bronze, cast. Persian or Mesopotamian, XII–XIII Cent. Unpublished. Acquired in Ardabil.
D. 4⅜ in.: 11·1 cm. *Bought* 1904.

5b    INKWELL, bronze, engraved and inlaid with silver and copper. Persian, XII Cent. Unpublished. The inscriptions are benedictory.
H. 3⅞ in.: 9·8 cm. *Bought* 1939.

6 and 7    EWER, brass, engraved and inlaid with silver and some copper. Persian, about 1200 A.D. Lane-Poole, p. 179. Details of the ornament on this and the companion piece in the Museum may be found in M. Lanci: *Trattato delle simboliche rappresentanze arabiche*, Paris, 1845–6, T. XXVIII–XXX.
H. 15¾ in.: 40 cm. *Bought* 1848.

8 and 29a    VASE, brass, engraved and inlaid with silver. Persian, about 1200 A.D. E. Piot: *Cabinet de l'amateur*, Paris, 1844, T. III, pp. 385–392. The handle, a later addition, has been removed.
H. 6 in.: 15·3 cm. *Bought* 1885.

9   FLASK, bronze, engraved and inlaid with silver and some copper. East Persian, XIII Cent. The inscriptions are benedictory. Acquired in Rawalpindi, Punjab.
H. 12⅜ in.: 31·4 cm. *Given by A. W. Franks, 1883.*

10   BUCKET, brass, engraved and inlaid with copper. East Persian, XIII Cent. The inscriptions are benedictory. Acquired in India.
H. (to top of handle) 11⅝ in.: 29·5 cm. *Given by A. W. Franks, 1885.*

11   MORTAR, bronze, engraved and inlaid with silver and copper. Mongol(?), XIII Cent. Unpublished. The Arabic inscription is benedictory. The Chinese inscription on the base, in a form of seal character, reads: Chih Pao Yung Chih(?) "Use this only (as a) treasure".
H. 4⅝ in.: 11·7 cm. *Given by A. W. Franks, 1883.*

12 and 13   EWER, brass, engraved and inlaid with silver and copper. Made at Mosul by Shuja' ibn Man'a of Mosul in A.H. 629/1232 A.D. Wiet, No. 44. A candlestick in the Harari Collection (Wiet, No. 66) is signed by an assistant of Shuja' of Mosul, the engraver.
H. 12 in.: 30·4 cm. *Bought 1866 (Blacas Collection).*

14 and 15 (a and b)   WRITING BOX, brass, engraved and inlaid with silver and copper. North Mesopotamian, Mosul, first half XIII Cent. Lane-Poole, p. 184, No. 12. The inscriptions are benedictory and in praise of learning and penmanship. Migeon (Vol. II, p. 80 and fig. 256), confused by the four writing boxes mentioned by Lane-Poole, states that this piece bears the name of the Mamluk Sultan Sha'ban. The error is continued in Wiet, No. 222.
L. 14½ in.: 36·8 cm. *Given by A. W. Franks, 1884.*

15c   INCENSE-BURNER, brass, pierced and inlaid with silver. North Mesopotamian, Mosul, dated A.H. 641/1243–4 A.D. Lane-Poole, p. 171; Wiet, No. 52.
H. 7¾ in.: 19·6 cm. *Henderson Bequest (678), 1878.*

16 and 17   ASTRONOMICAL TABLE, brass, engraved and inlaid with silver and gold. Signed by Muhammad ibn Khutlukh of Mosul. North Mesopotamian, Mosul, dated A.H. 639/1241–2 A.D. Wiet, No. 50.
L. 13¼ in.: 33·7 cm. *Bought 1888.*

18   BOX, brass, engraved and inlaid with silver. Inscribed with name of Badr al-din Lulu. North Mesopotamian, Mosul, 1233–59 A.D. Lane-Poole, p. 172; Wiet, No. 74. Migeon (Vol. II, Fig. 237) illustrates a silver and copper inlaid box with Christian figures in the Victoria and Albert Museum.
H. 4 in.: 10·2 cm. *Henderson Bequest (674), 1878.*

19 and 20   ASTROLABE, brass, engraved and inlaid with silver and copper. Made at Cairo by 'Abd al-Karim, of Cairo, the astrolabist, follower of al-Malik al Ashraf, al-Malik al Mu'izz and Shihab (al-din) in A.H. 633/1236 A.D. Lane-Poole, p. 177; van Berchem, p. 32, Note 2; Wiet, No. 45. R. T. Gunther: *Astrolabes of the World*, Oxford, 1932, Vol. I, p. 236.
H. 15½ in.: 39·4 cm. *Bought 1855.*

21 INCENSE-BURNER, brass, pierced and inlaid with silver and some gold. Syrian, middle XIII Cent. M. Aga-Oglu: "About a type of Islamic Incense-burner", *The Art Bulletin*, March, 1945, Vol. XXVII, No. 1, p. 33.

H. 8 in.: 20·3 cm. *Henderson Bequest* (679), 1878.

22 HANDWARMER, brass, pierced and inlaid with silver. Inscribed with name of Badr al-din Baysari. Syrian, 1264–79 A.D. Lane-Poole, p. 174; Wiet, No. 87; L. A. Mayer: *Saracenic Heraldry*, Oxford, 1933, p. 112. Migeon (Vol. II, p.70) is in error in stating that the handwarmer is dated A.H. 670/1271 A.D.

D. 7¼ in.: 18·4 cm. *Henderson Bequest* (682), 1878.

23 DETAIL OF SALVER, brass, inlaid with silver and some gold. Syrian, second half of XIII Cent. The inscriptions, where legible, are benedictory. Migeon (Vol. II, p. 80 and Fig. 255) is in error in stating that the salver bears the name of the Mamluk sultan Nasir Faraj (1398–1412). The error is continued in Wiet, No. 302.

D. of centre medallion, 5⅜ in.: 13·6 cm. *Henderson Bequest* (706), 1878.

24 CANDLESTICK, brass, inlaid with silver. Syrian, late XIII Cent. Unpublished. The inscriptions are benedictory.

H. 11¾ in.: 29·8 cm. *Bought 1866 (Blacas Collection)*.

25 WRITING-BOX, brass, inlaid with silver and gold. Syrian, first half of XIV Cent. Lane-Poole, p. 184, No. 13.

L. 8¾ in.: 22·3 cm. *Burges Bequest* (19), 1881.

26a INCENSE-BURNER, brass, pierced and inlaid with silver. Syrian, first half XIV Cent. Lane-Poole, p. 177, No. 6.

H. 7⅜ in.: 18·7 cm. *Henderson Bequest* (681), 1878.

26b BOX, brass. inlaid with silver and gold. Inscribed with name of Ahmad, overseer to the Amir Muhammad ibn Satilmish al-Jalali. Egyptian, early XIV Cent. Lane-Poole, p. 193; Wiet, No. 237; L. A. Mayer: op. cit., p. 48.

H. 3⅞ in.: 9·8 cm. *Bought 1866 (Blacas Collection)*.

27 WRITING-BOX, brass, inlaid with silver and gold. Egyptian, first half XIV Cent. Lane-Poole, p. 184, No. 14, as corrected by van Berchem, p. 32, Note 2.

L. 12⅛ in.: 30·7 cm. *Burges Bequest* (20), 1881.

28 BASIN, brass, inlaid with silver and some gold. Inscribed with name of the Mamluk Sultan Nasir al-din Muhammad ibn Kalaun (1293–4, 1308 and 1309–40 A.D.). Egyptian, first half XIV Cent. Lane-Poole, p. 190; Wiet, No. 183.

D. 21⅛ in.: 53·6 cm. *Bought 1851*.

29b BASE OF EWER, brass, inlaid with silver and gold. Egyptian, first half XIV Cent. *Archæological Journal*, 1859, XVI, p. 362. Inscriptions contain series of Mamluk titles.

D. of base 3⅝ in.: 9·2 cm. *Bought 1887 (Alexander Nesbitt Collection)*.

30 HELMET, steel, parcel-gilt and inlaid with silver. Egyptian, XV Cent. Inscriptions are benedictory and eulogistic.

H. 10¾ in.: 27·3 cm. *Tower Collection* (15–685).

31  FOOD-BOX, brass, engraved. Egyptian, XVI Cent. Unpublished.
H. 7¼ in.: 18·4 cm. *Bought* 1908.

32 and 33  WRITING-BOX, brass, inlaid with silver and gold. Signed by Mahmud ibn Sunqur. Persian(?), dated A.H. 680/1281 A.D. The artist does not sign himself "of Baghdad" as in Wiet, No. 93.
L. 7¾ in.: 19·7 cm. *Bought* 1891 (*Rhode Hawkins Collection*).

34  GOBLET, brass, inlaid with silver. Persian, XIV Cent. The Persian verses round the rim refer to the goblet; the Arabic inscription on the foot is benedictory.
H. 5 in.: 12·7 cm. *Bought* 1891 (*Rhode Hawkins Collection*).

35  CANDLESTICK, brass, inlaid with silver. Persian, XIV Cent. Unpublished. The inscriptions are benedictory. The shoulder is misshapen.
H. 12¼ in.: 31·1 cm. *Bought* 1948.

36  BOWL, brass, inlaid with silver and gold. Persian, late XIV Cent. The inscription is eulogistic.
D. 9⅜ in.: 23·8 cm. *Given by the Friends of the British Museum*, 1901.

37  CASKET, brass, inlaid with silver and gold. Persian, late XIV Cent.
H. 5 in.: 12·7 cm. *Henderson Bequest* (676), 1878.

38a  EWER, copper, gilt and engraved. Persian, XVI Cent. Unpublished.
H. 7¾ in.: 19·7 cm. *Bought* 1897 (*from a Constantinople Collection*).

38b and 39  ARMPIECE AND HELMET, steel, carved and inlaid with gold. Inscribed with name of Shah 'Abbas I (1587–1629). Persian, dated A.H. 1035/1625–6 A.D. Migeon (Vol. I, p. 424) is in error in referring the R.H. armpiece in his Fig. 210 to Shah 'Abbas.
Armpiece: L. (Overall) 21½ in.: 54·6 cm. *Henderson Bequest* (771), 1878.
Helmet: H. (less mail) 10¾ in.: 27·3 cm. *Henderson Bequest* (772), 1878.

40  ASTROLABE, brass, engraved and inlaid with silver. Inscribed with name of Shah Husayn (1694–1722). Persian, dated A.H. 1124/1712 A.D. W. H. Morley: *Description of a Planispheric Astrolabe*, London, 1856, passim: R. T. Gunther: op. cit., Vol. I, p. 147.
H. 20⅞ in.: 53 cm. *Bought* 1753 (*Sloane Collection*).

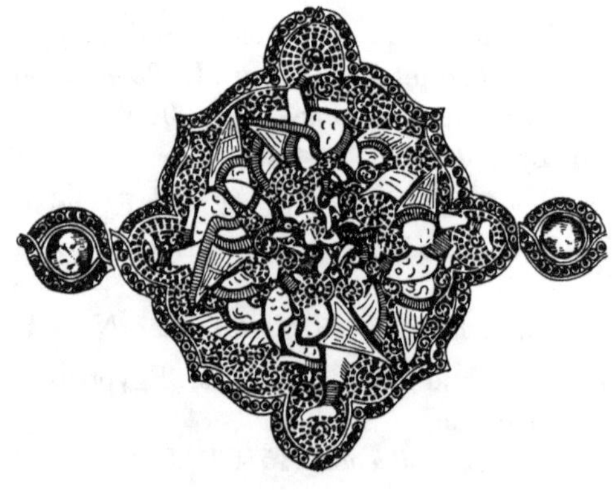

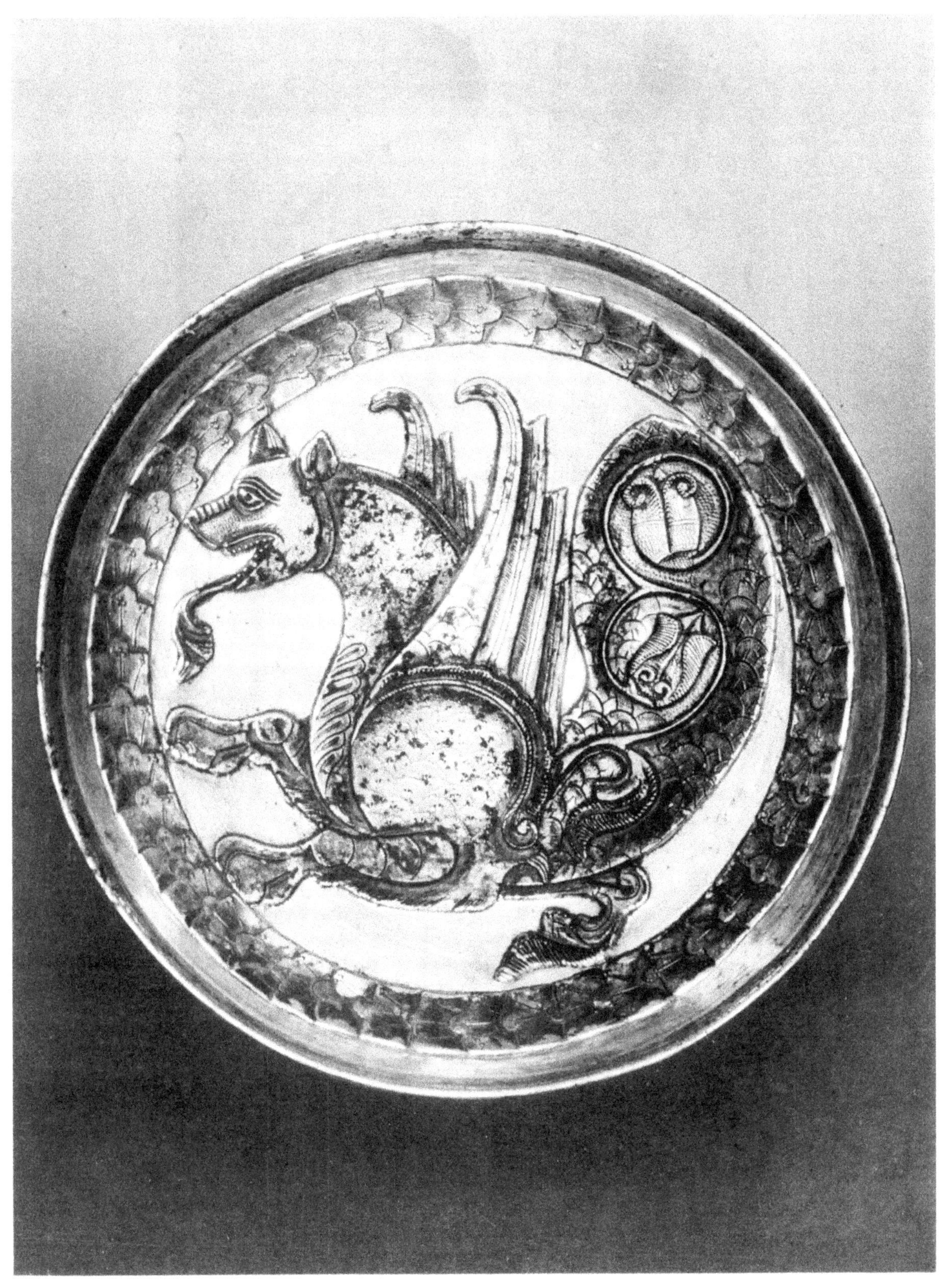

1. Silver dish, parcel gilt, *Sasanian or post-Sasanian*.

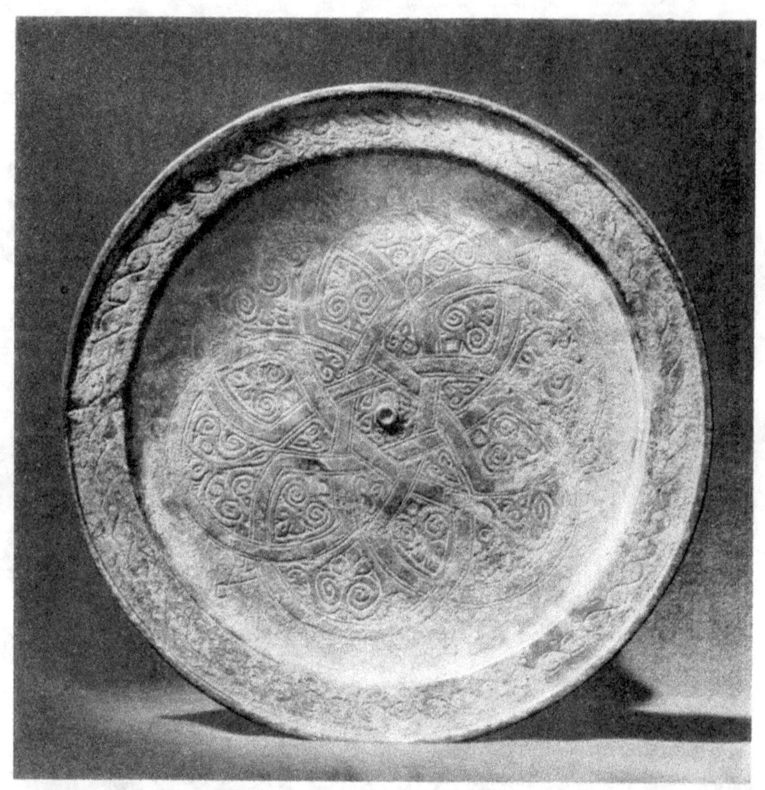

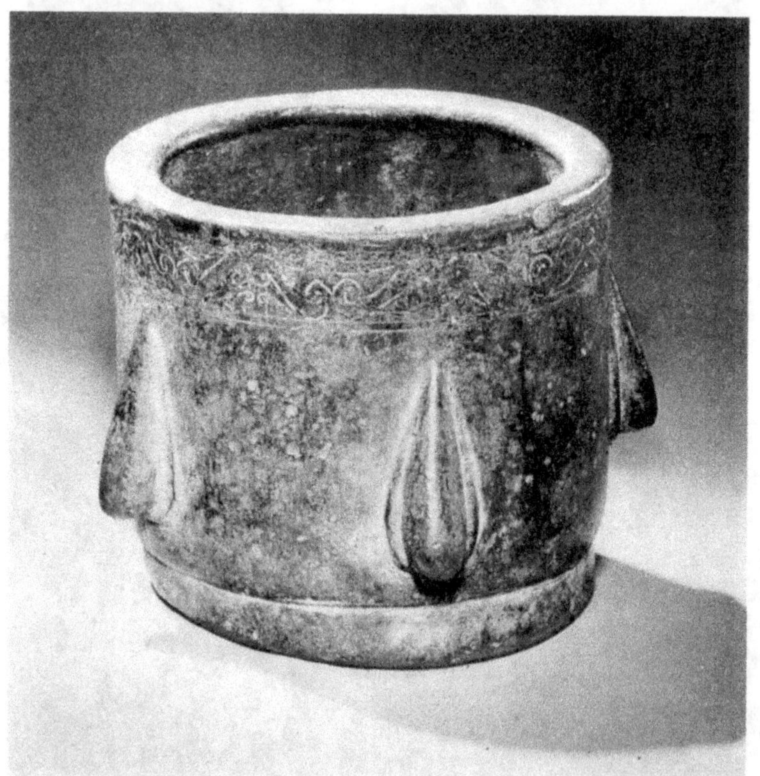

2(a). Bronze plate and 2(b) Bronze mortar. *Persian. X–XI Cent.*

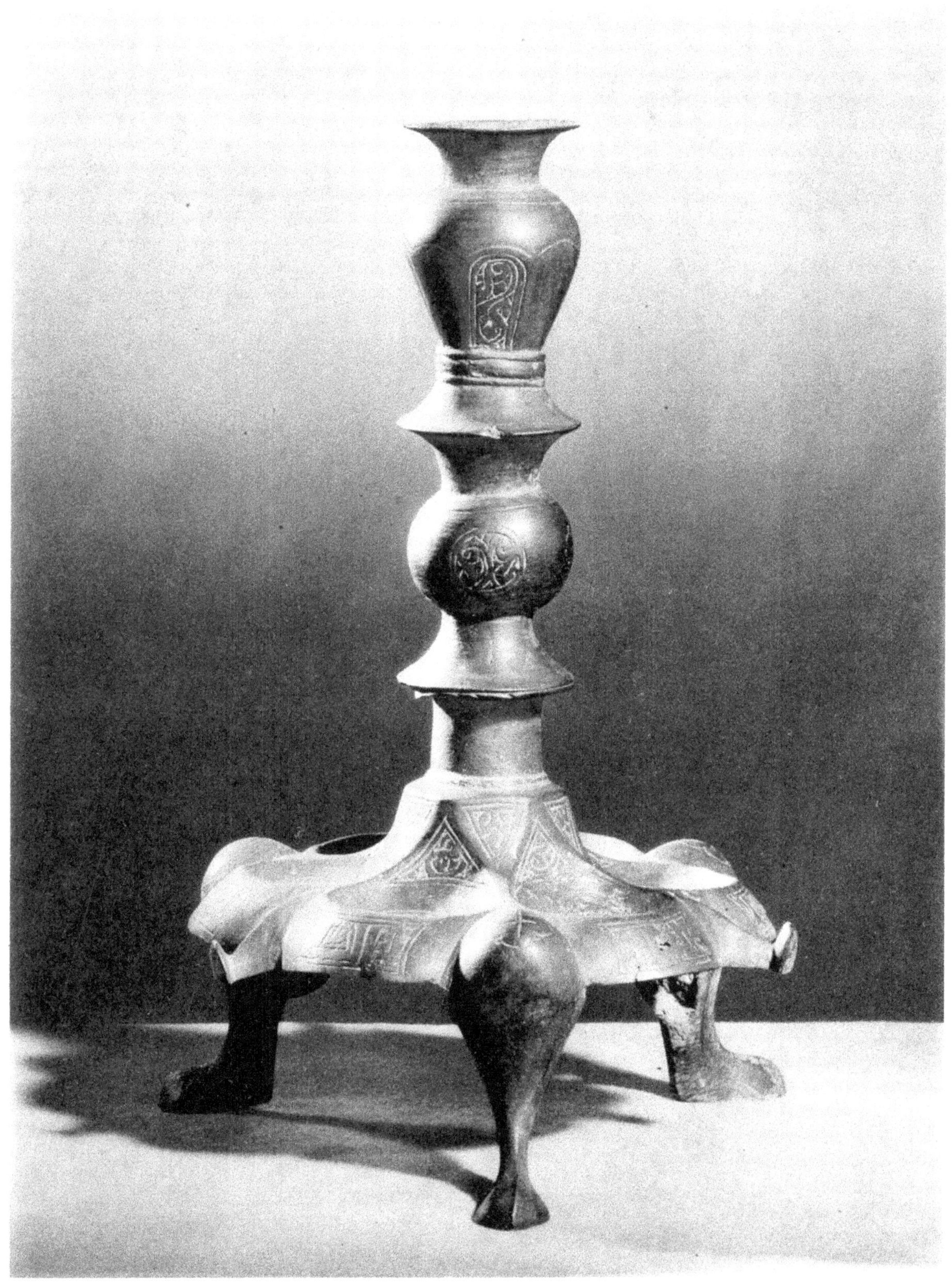

3. Bronze stand. *Persian. XII–XIII Cent.*

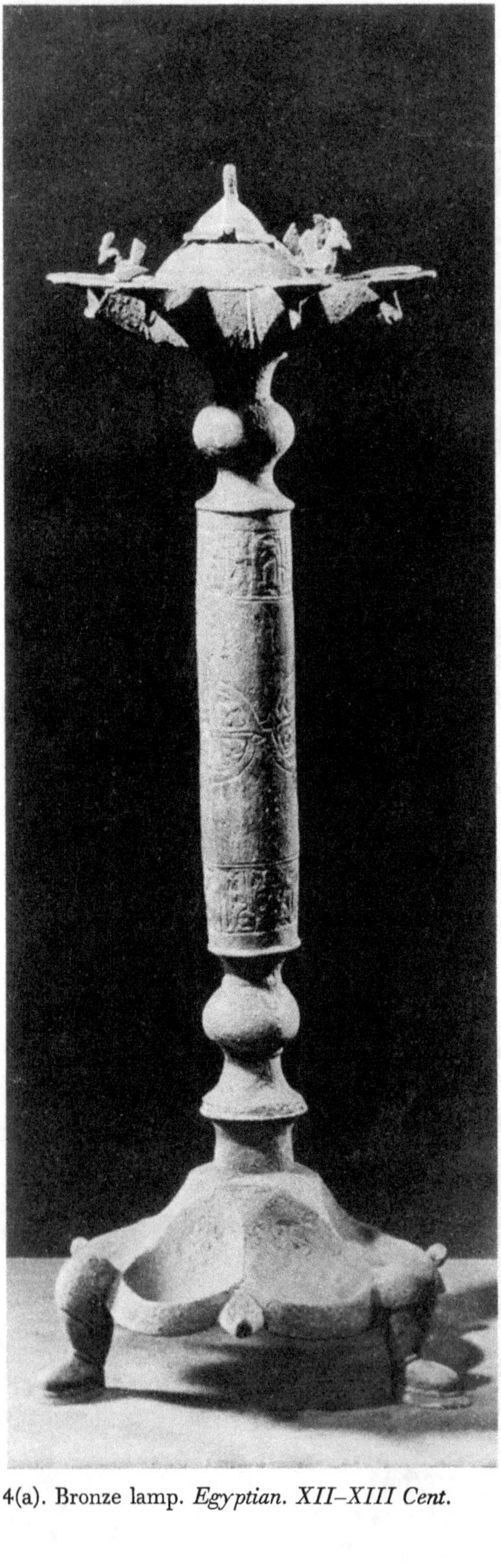

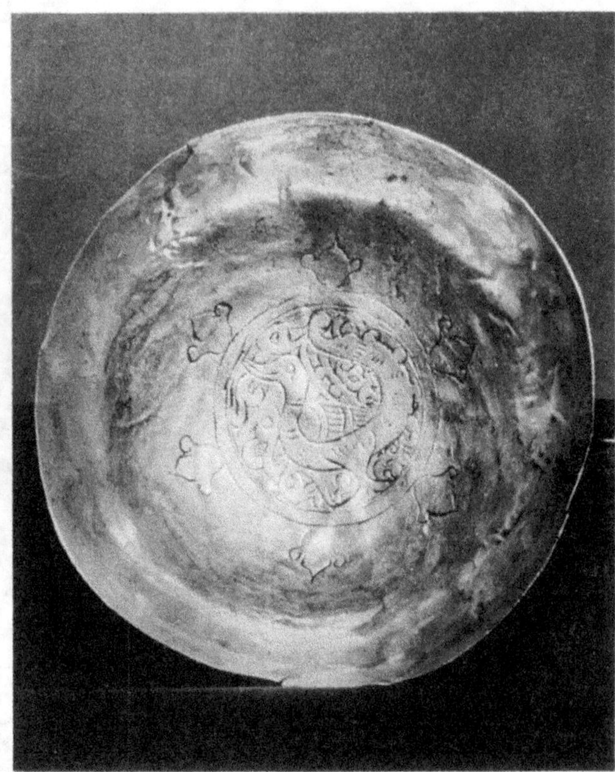

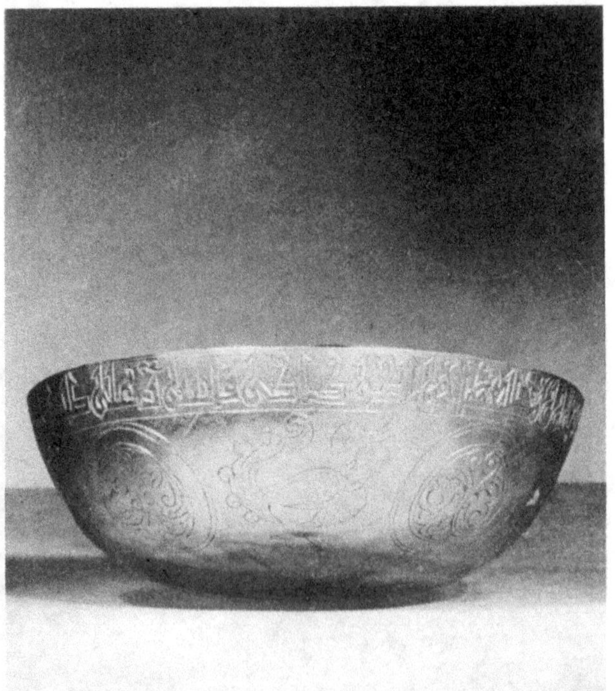

4(a). Bronze lamp. *Egyptian. XII–XIII Cent.*     4(b) and (c). Gold bowl. *Persian. XI–XII Cent.*

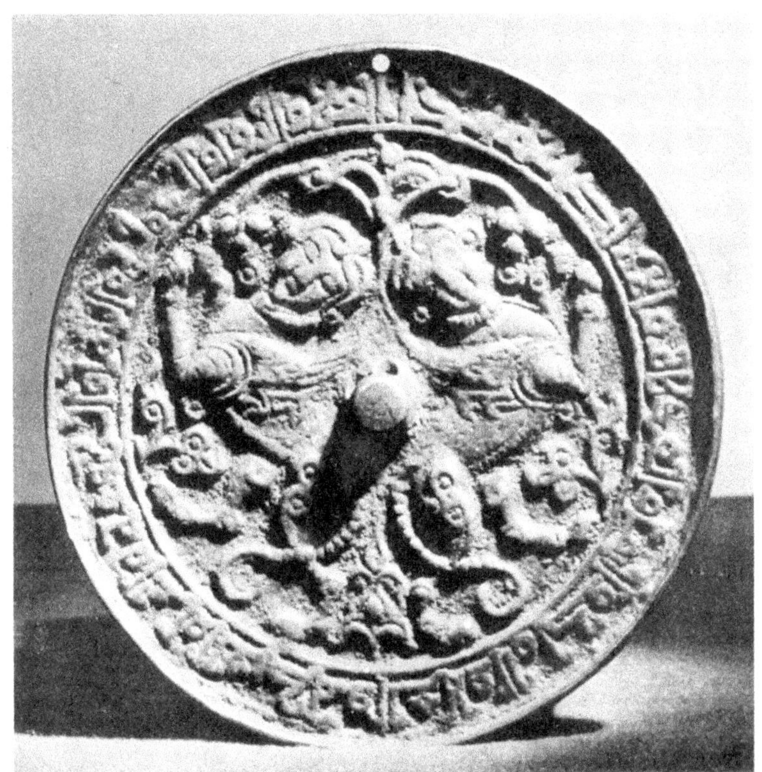

5(a). Bronze mirror. *Persian or Mesopotamian. XII–XIII Cent.*

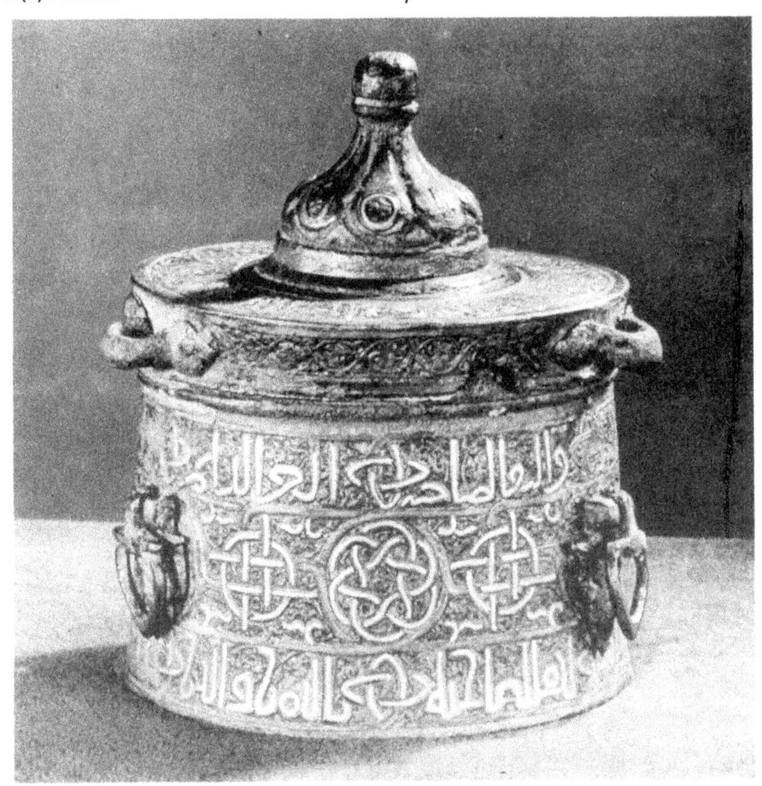

5(b). Bronze inkwell, inlaid. *Persian. XII Cent.*

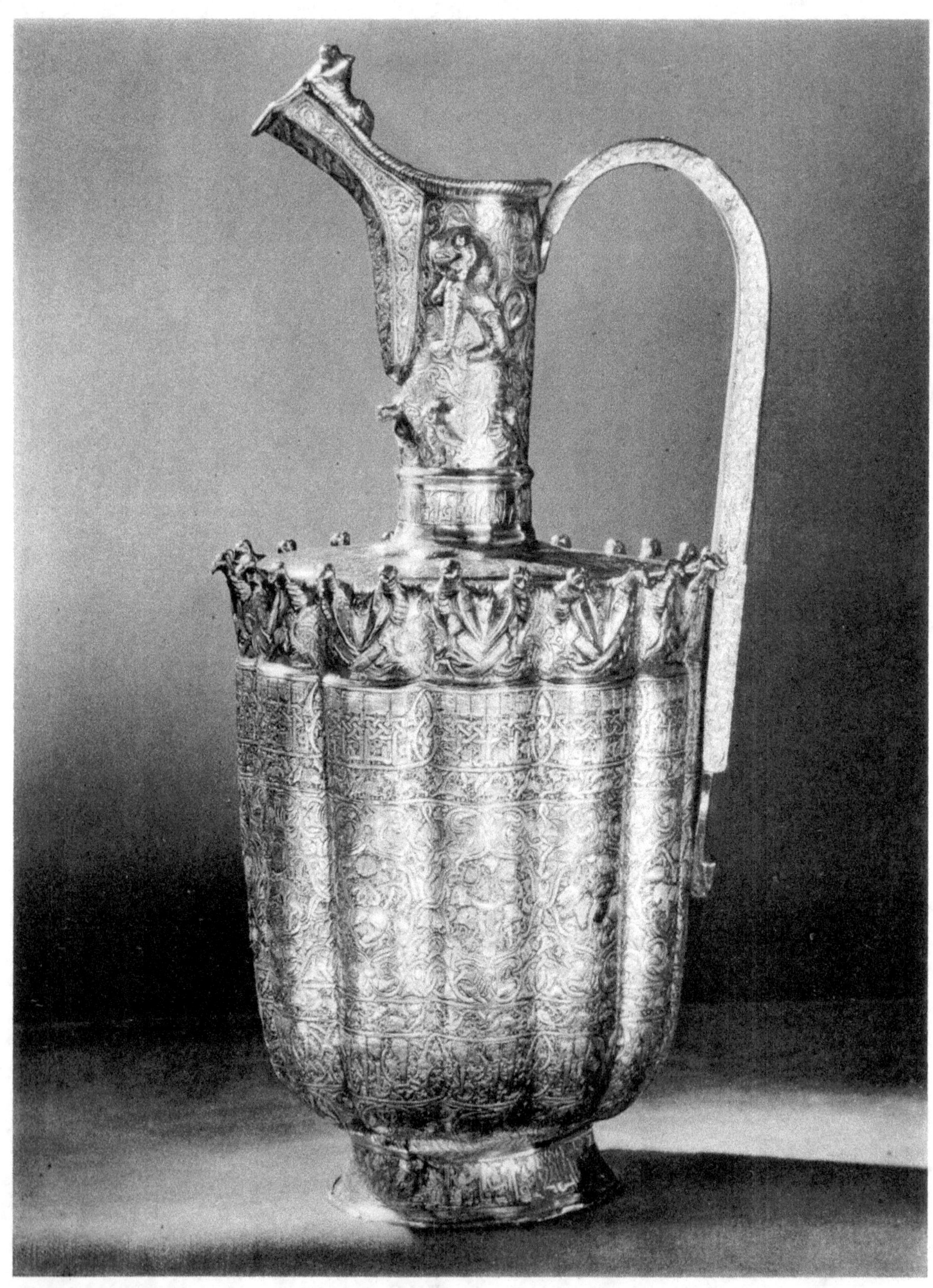

6 and 7. Brass ewer, inlaid. *Persian. About* 1200 *A.D.*

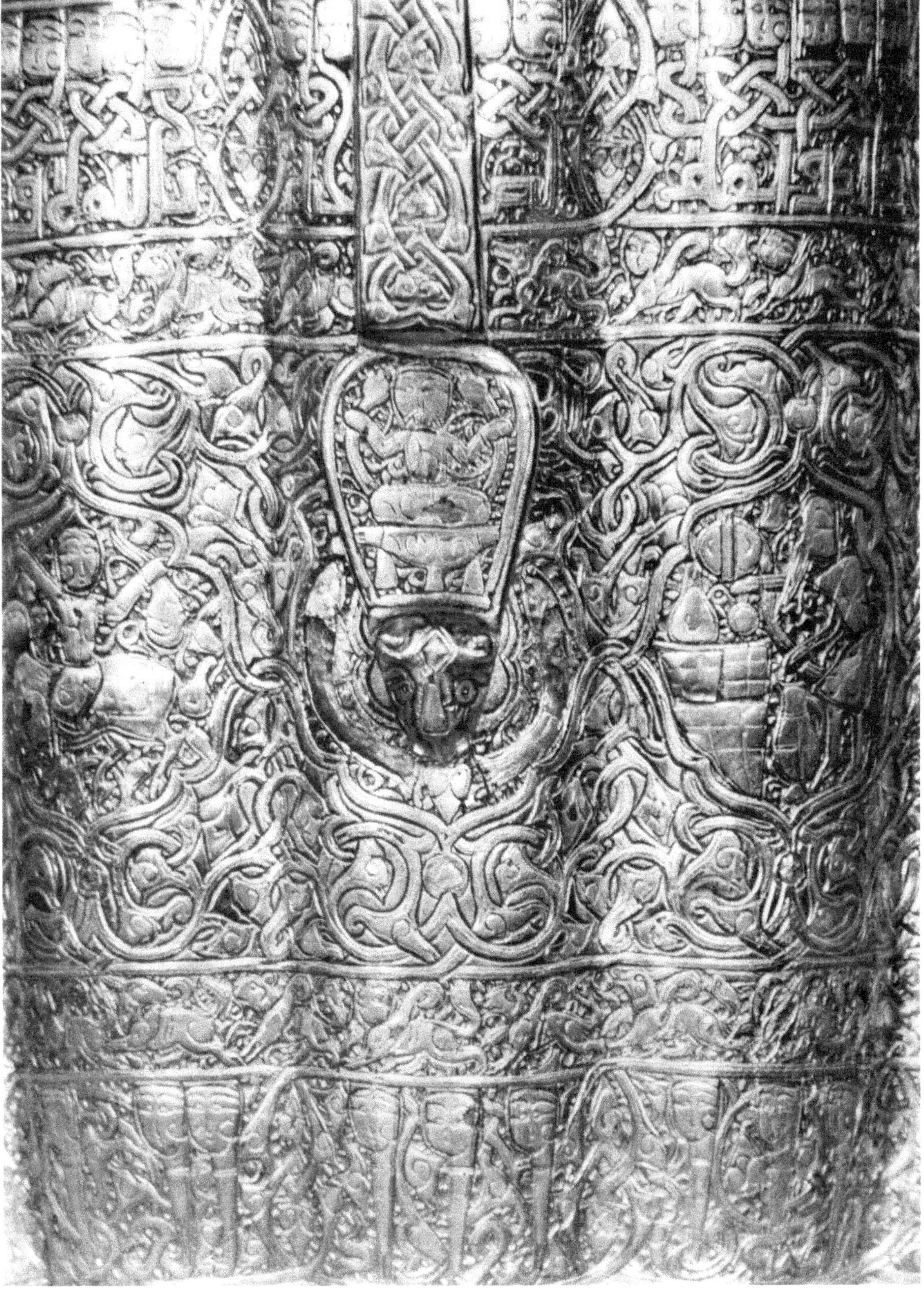

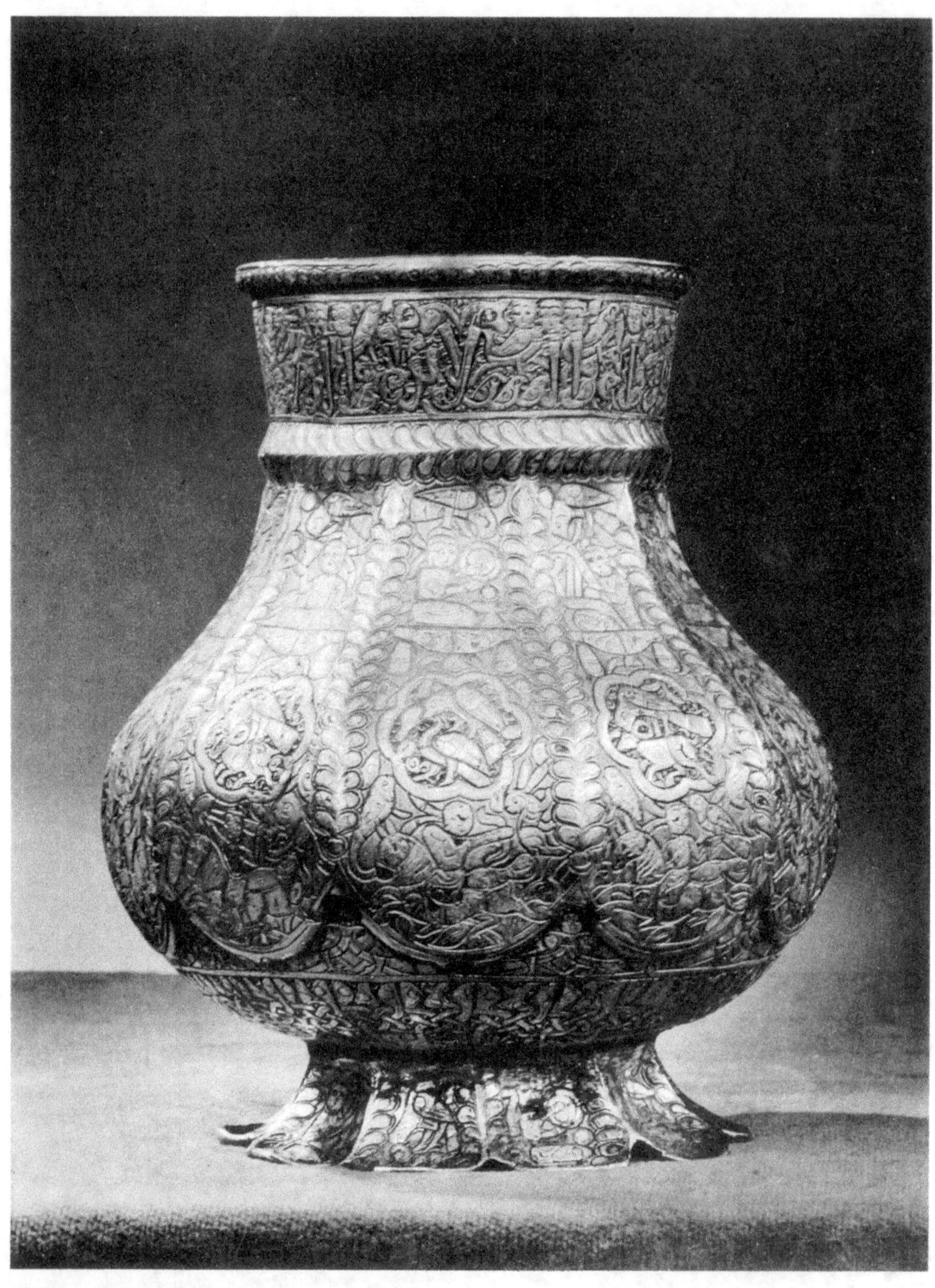

8. Brass vase, inlaid. *Persian. About* 1200 *A.D.*

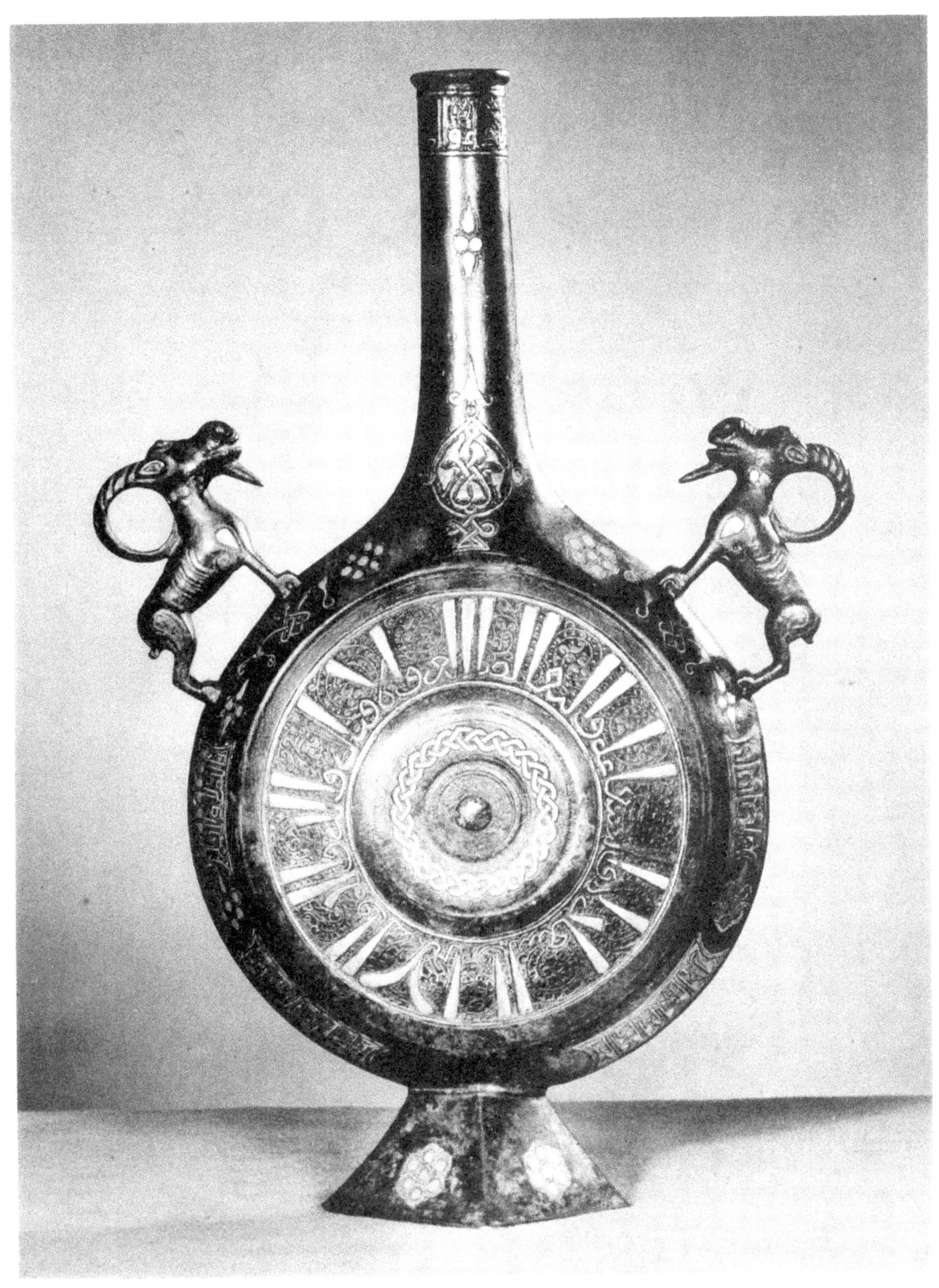

9. Bronze flask, inlaid. *East Persian. XIII Cent.*

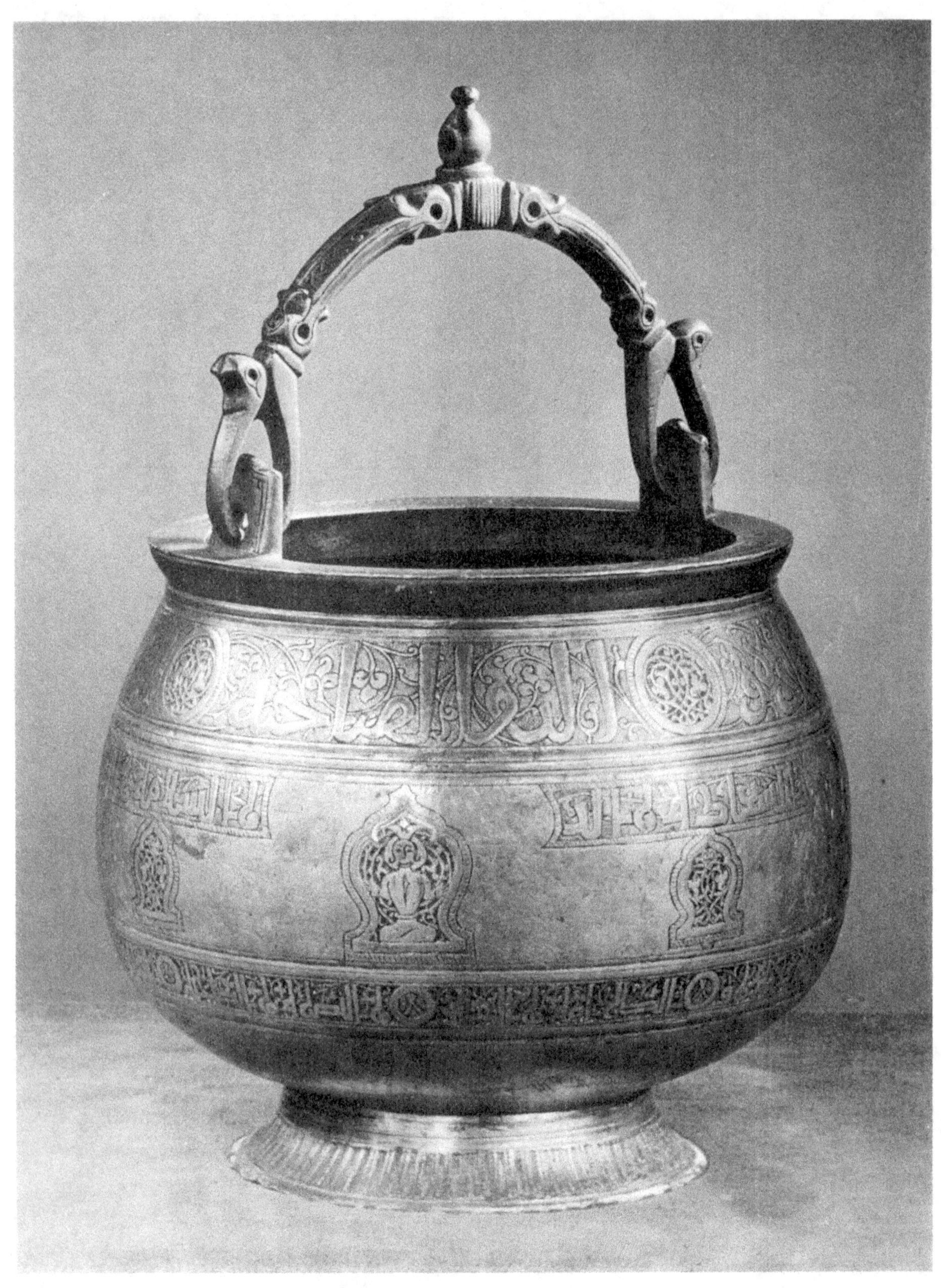

10. Brass bucket, inlaid. *East Persian. XIII Cent.*

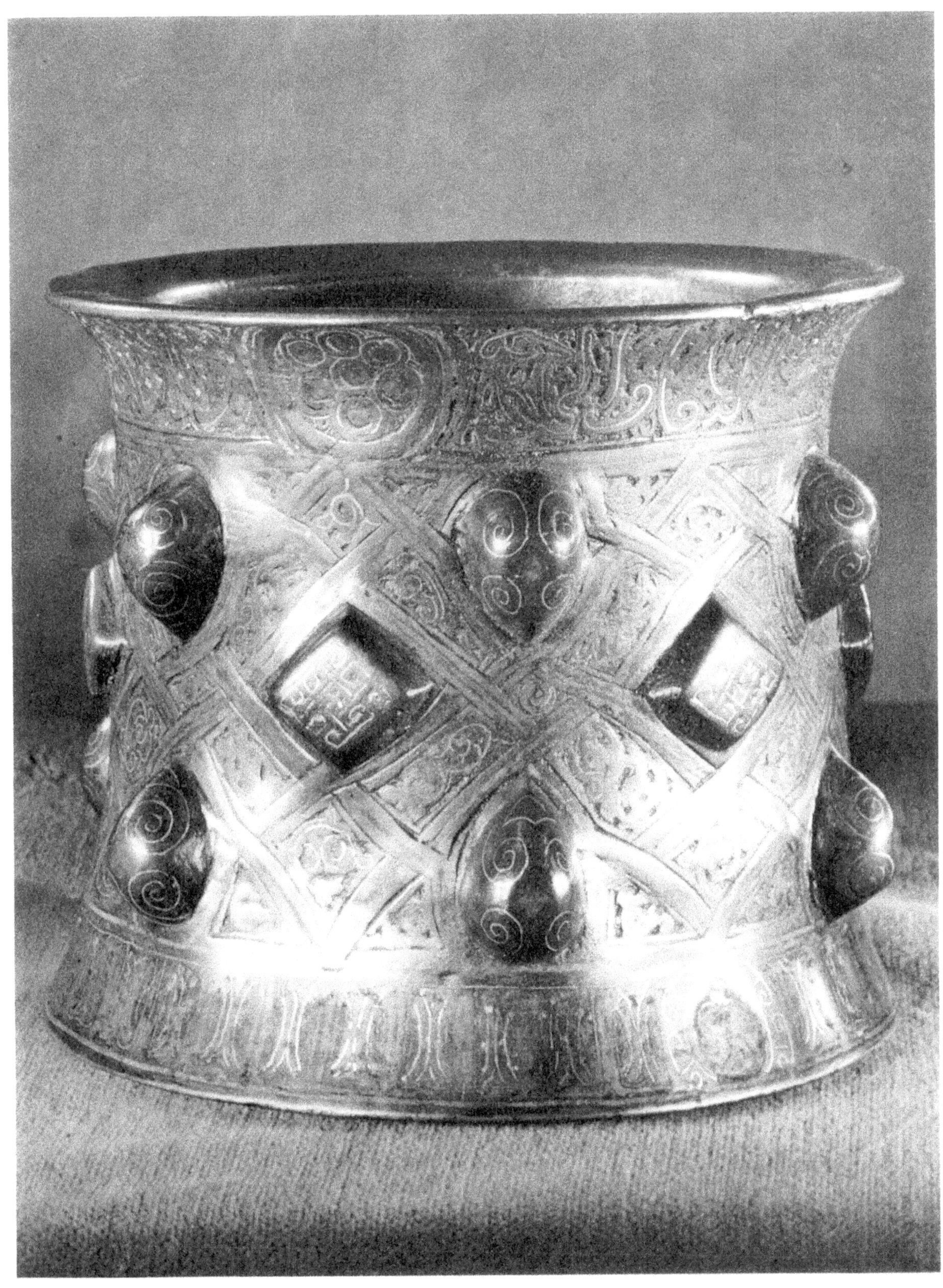

11. Bronze mortar, inlaid. *Mongol*(?). *XIII Cent.*

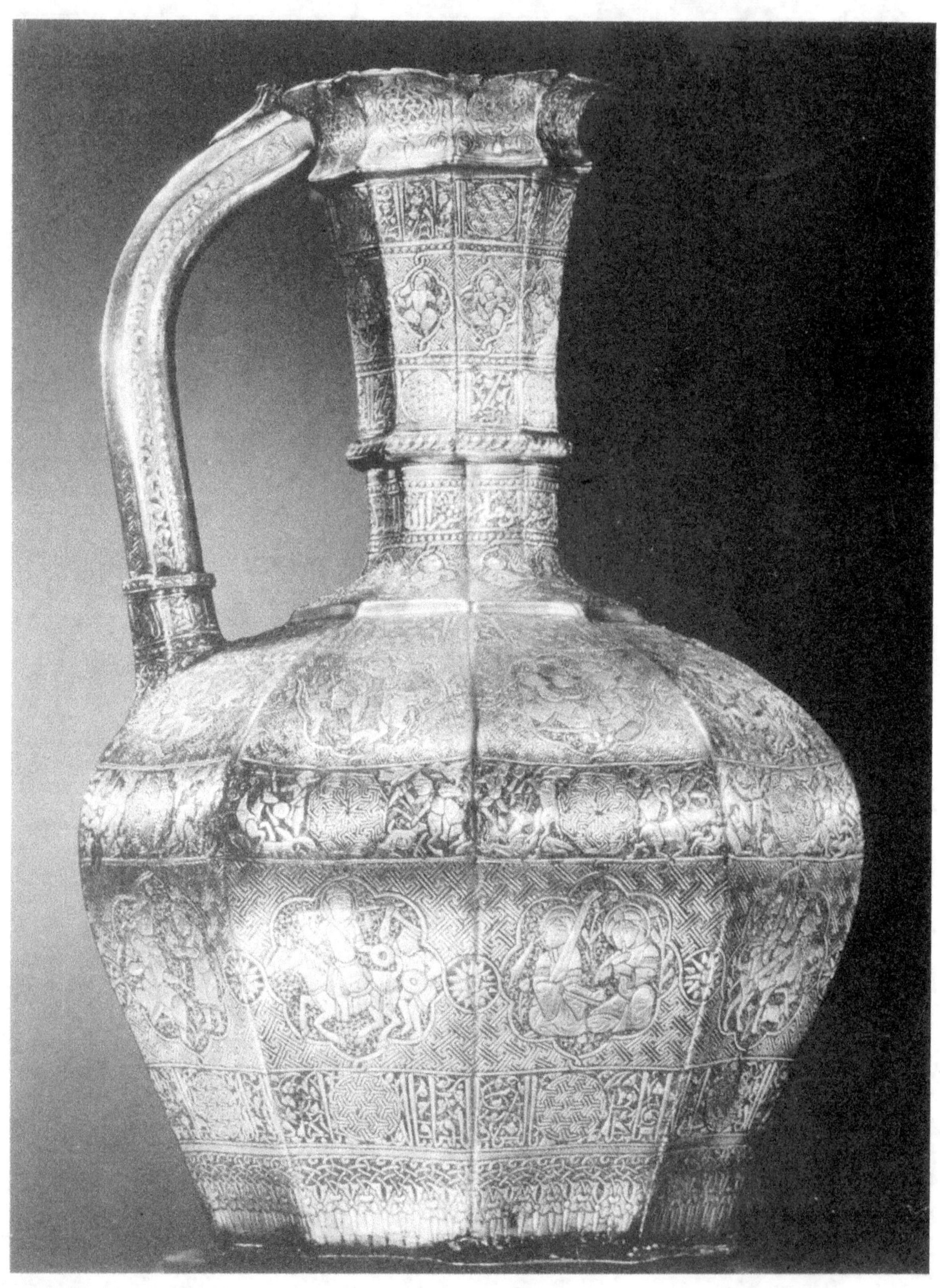

12. Brass ewer, inlaid. *North Mesopotamian, Mosul.* 1232 *A.D.*

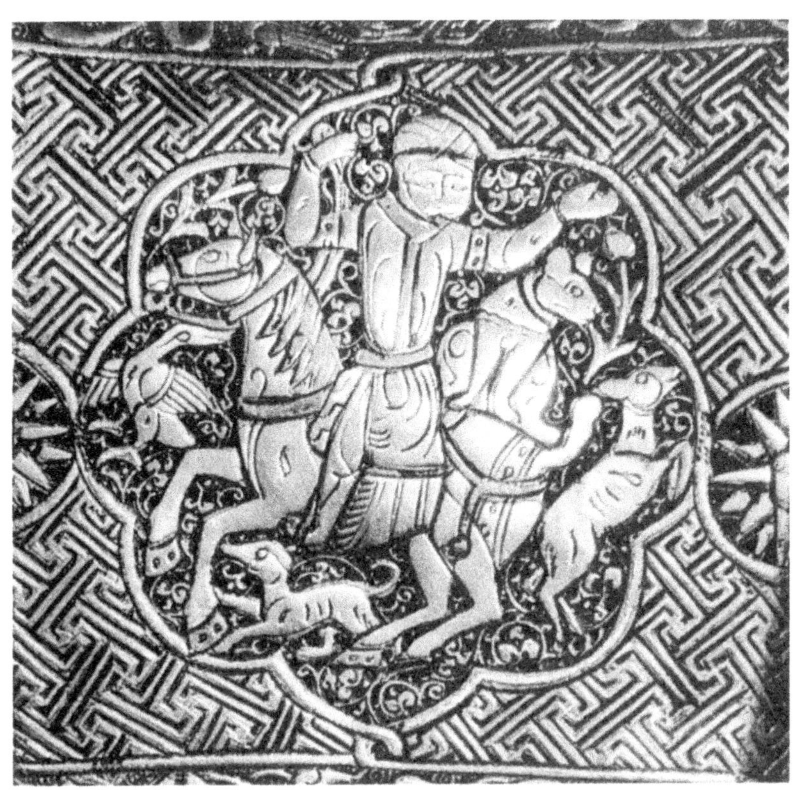

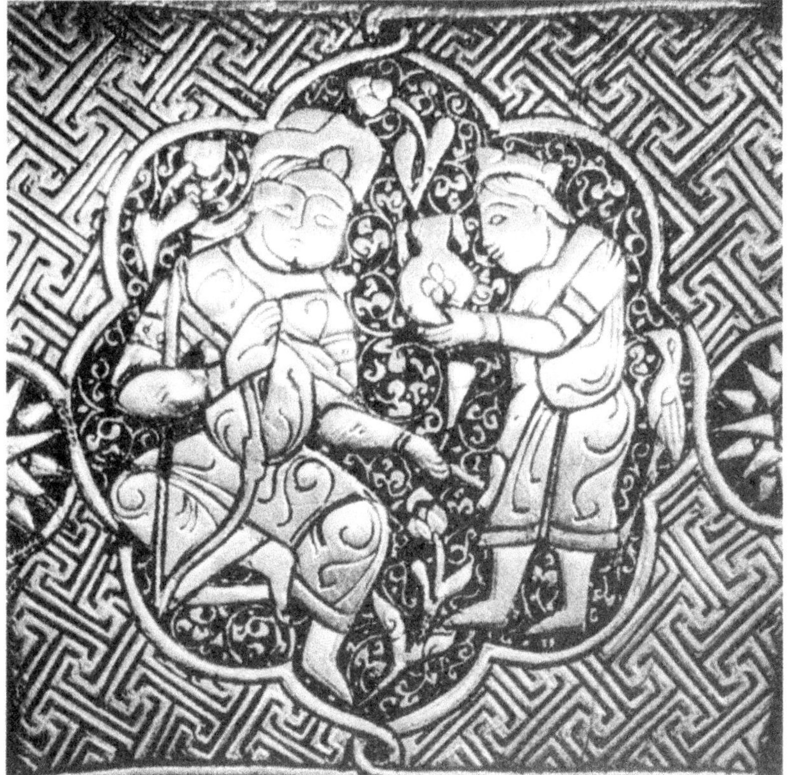

13. Details of ewer on Plate 12.

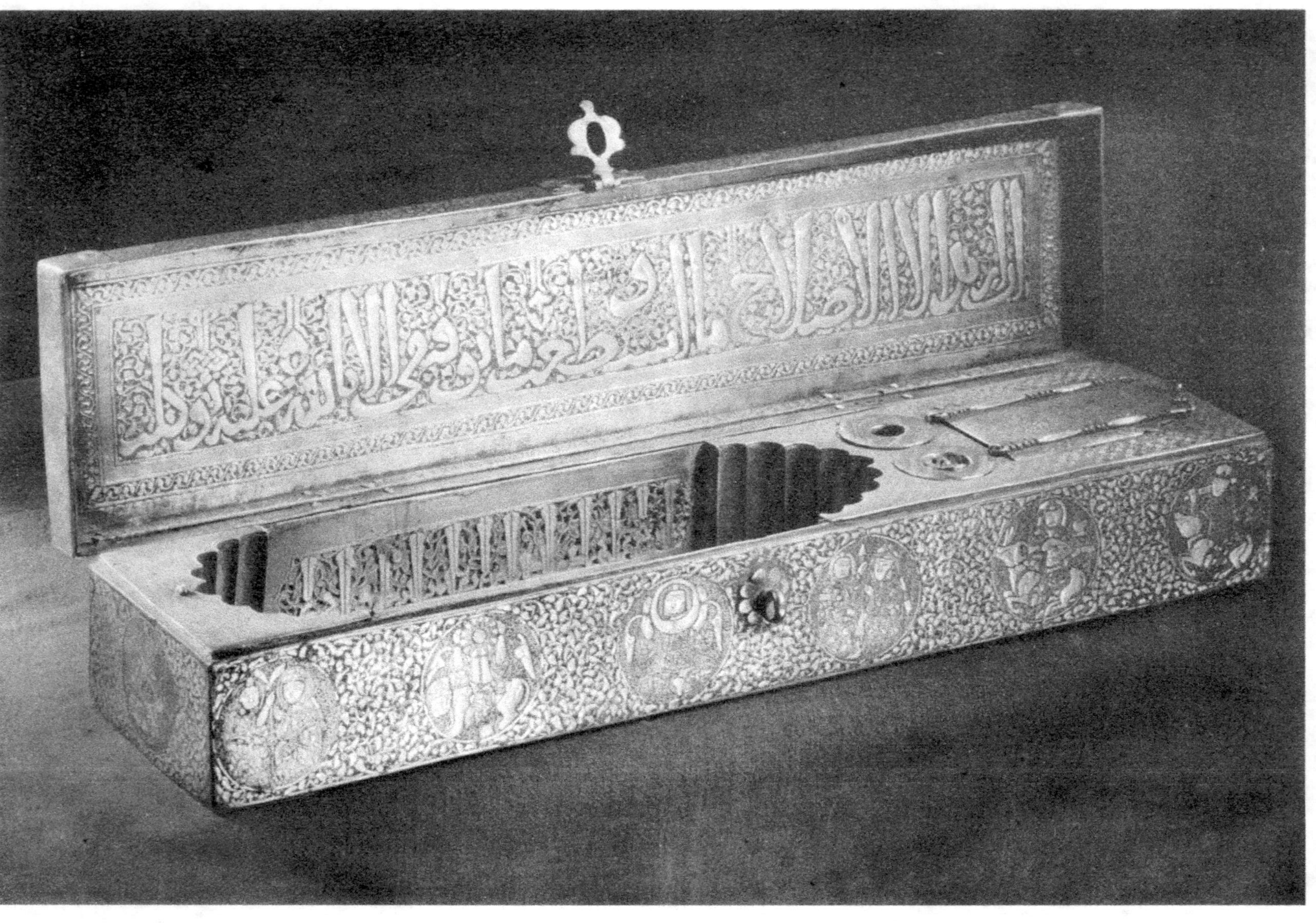

14. Brass writing-box, inlaid. *North Mesopotamian, Mosul. First half of XIII Cent.*

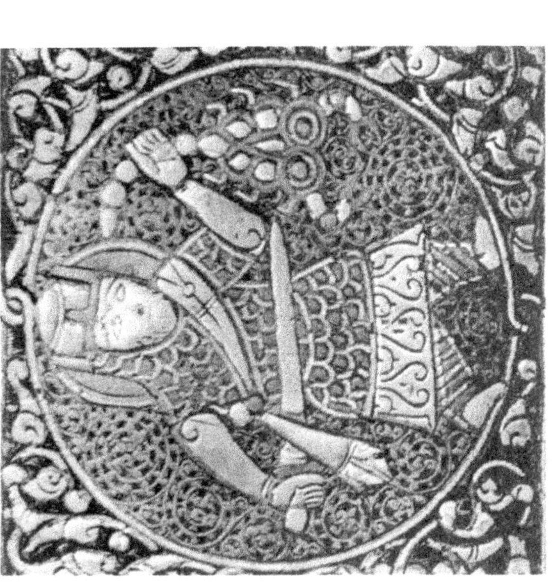

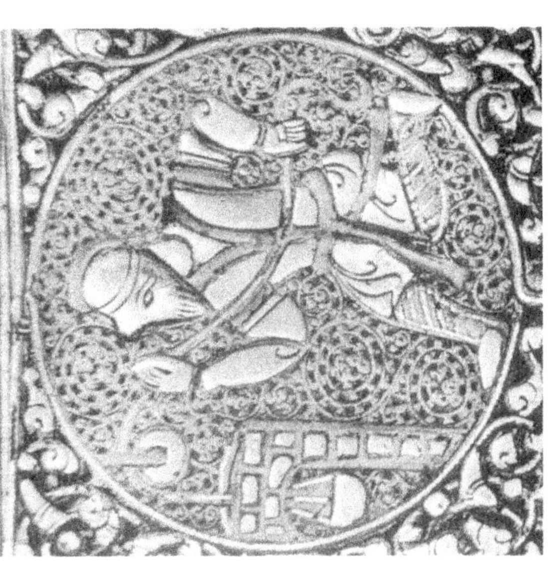

15(a) and (b). Details of writing-box on Plate 14.

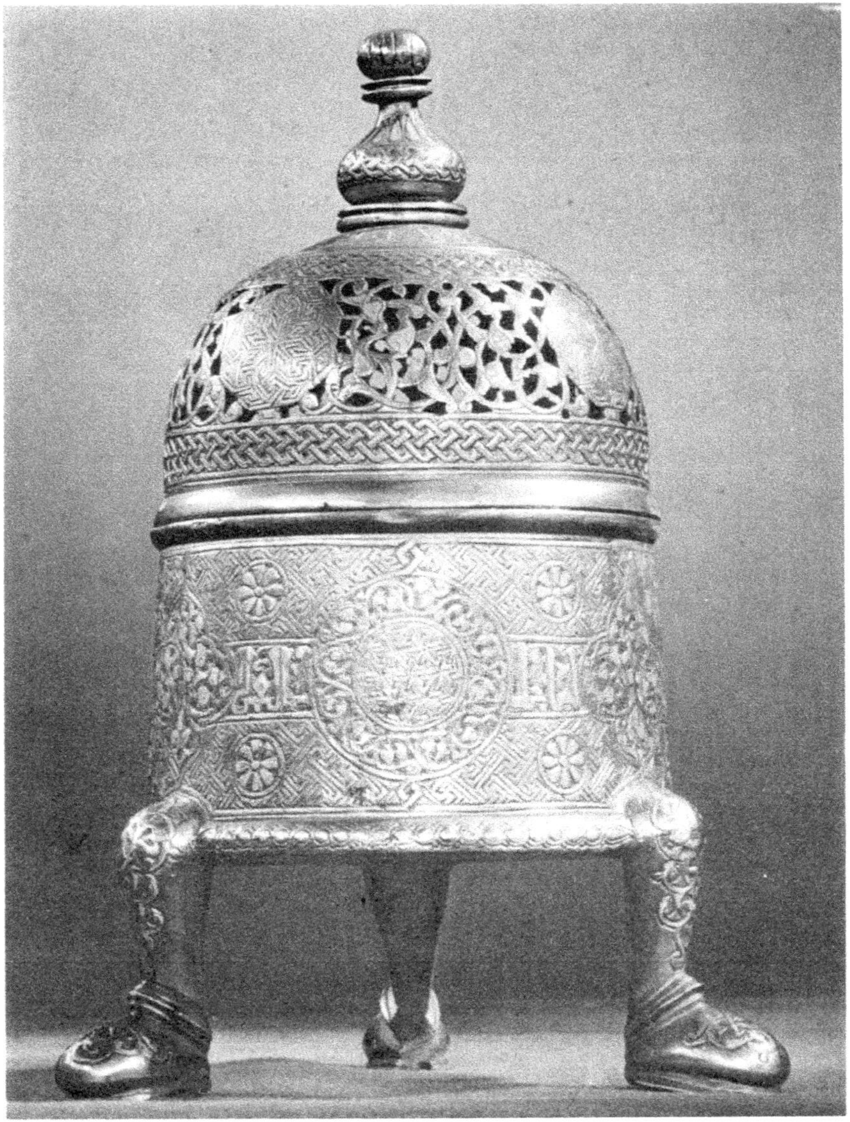

15(c). Brass incense-burner, inlaid. *North Mesopotamian, Mosul.* 1243-4 *A.D.*

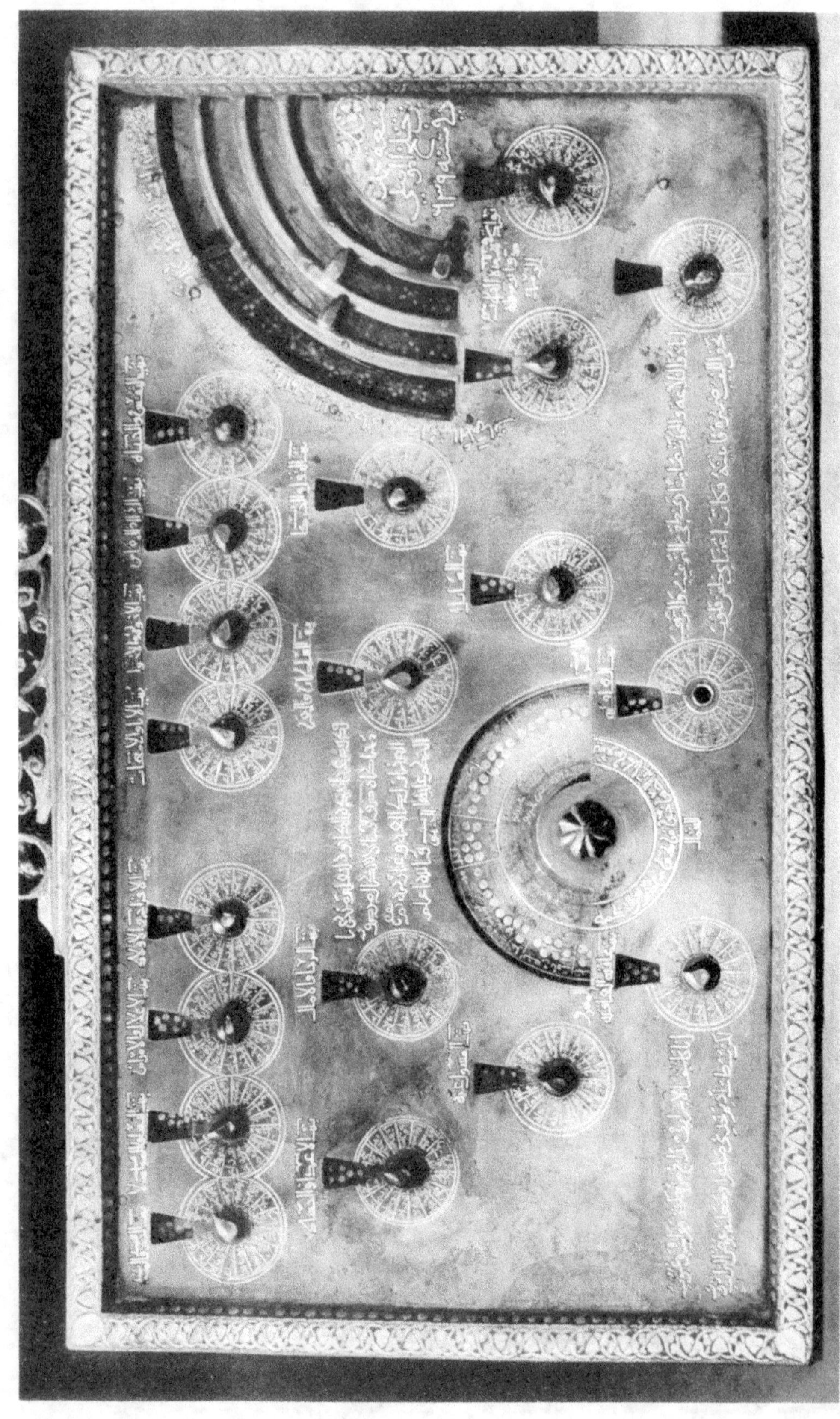

16. Brass astronomical table, inlaid. *North Mesopotamian, Mosul. 1241-2 A.D.*

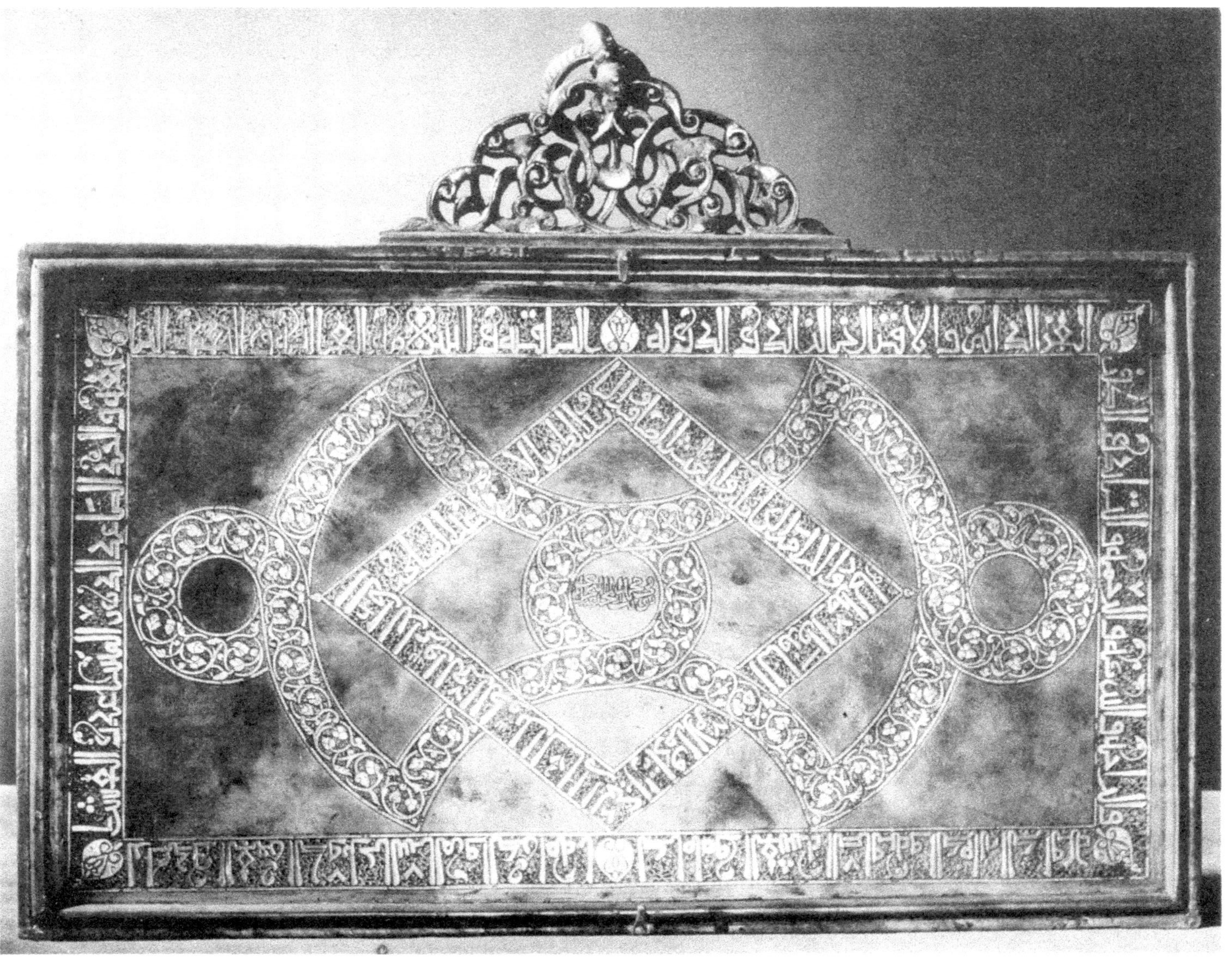

**17.** Reverse of astronomical table on Plate 16.

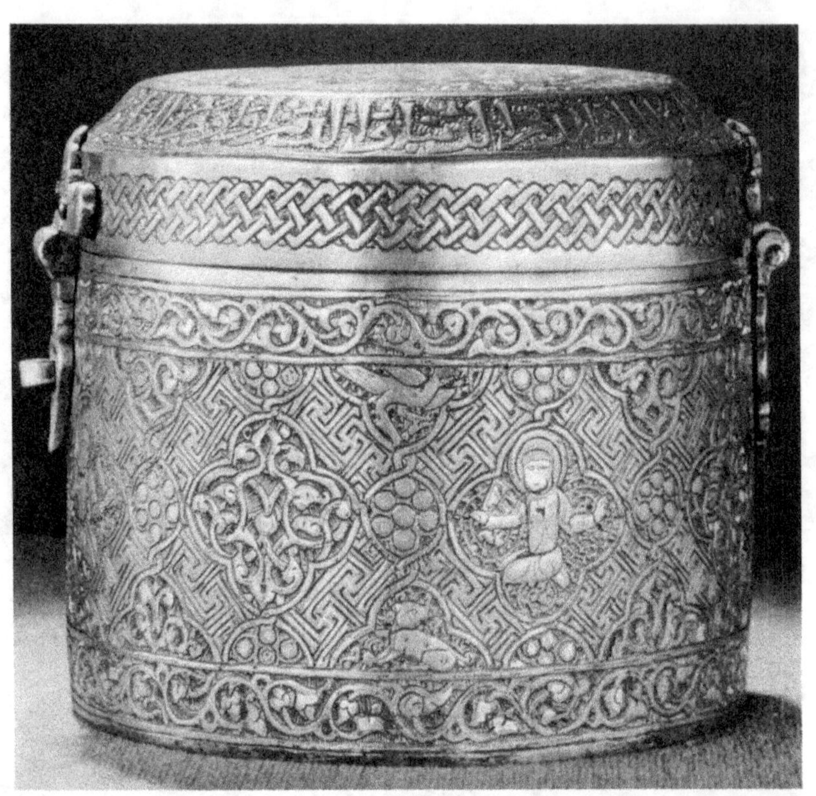

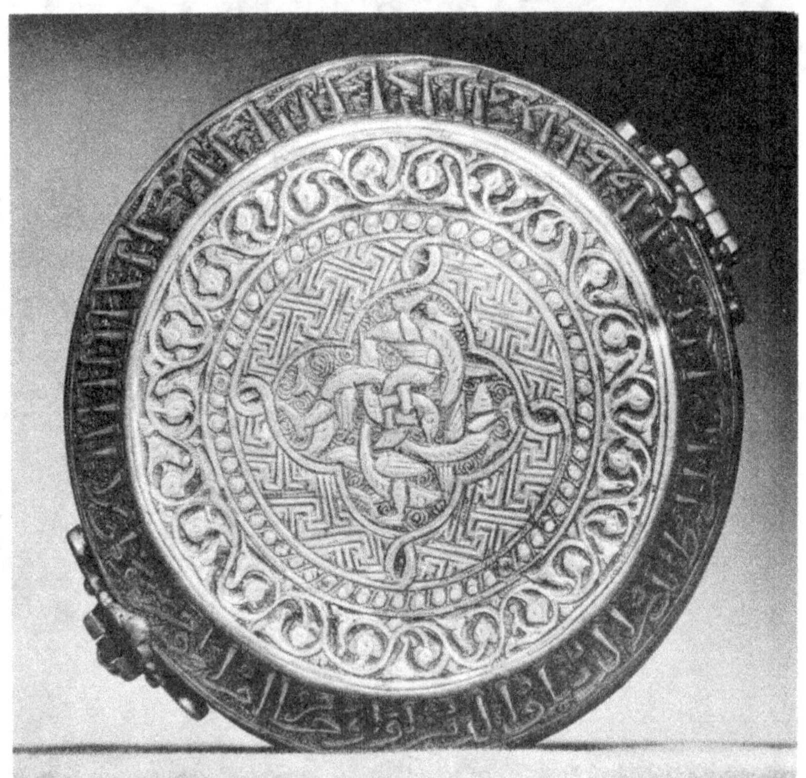

18. Brass box, inlaid. *North Mesopotamian, Mosul. 1233–59 A.D.*

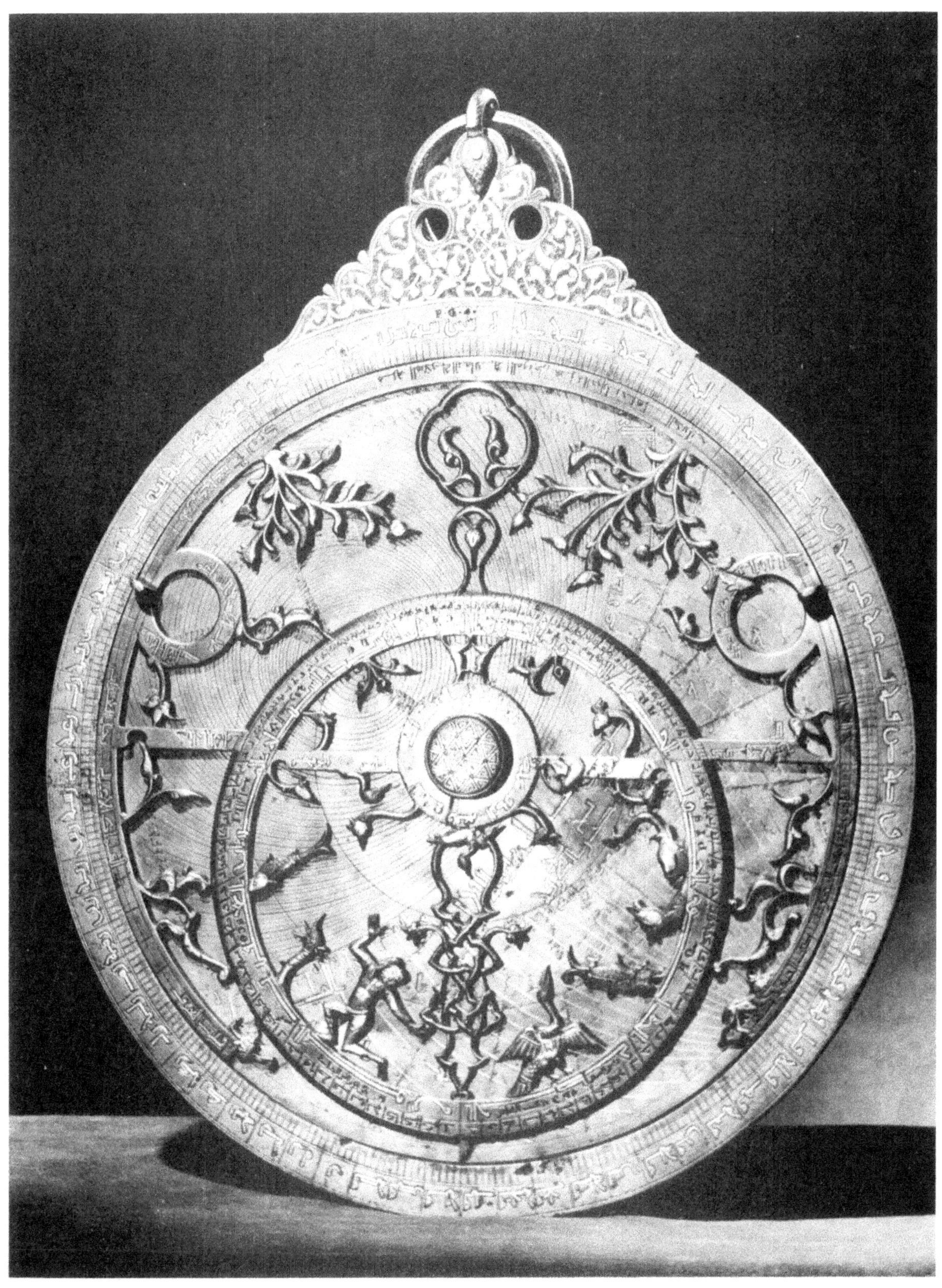

19. Brass astrolabe, inlaid. *Egyptian.* 1236 *A.D.*

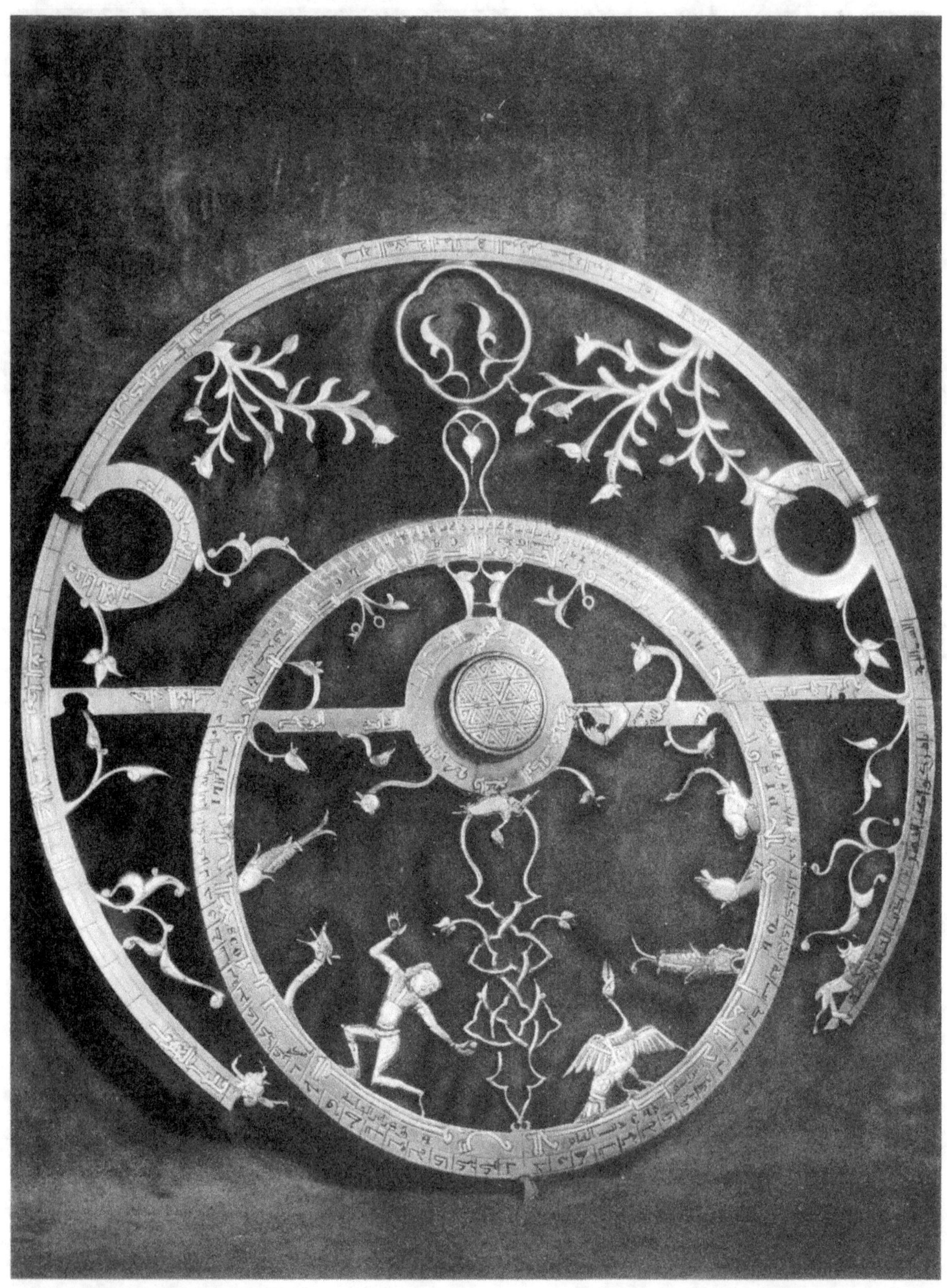

20. Detail of astrolabe on Plate 19.

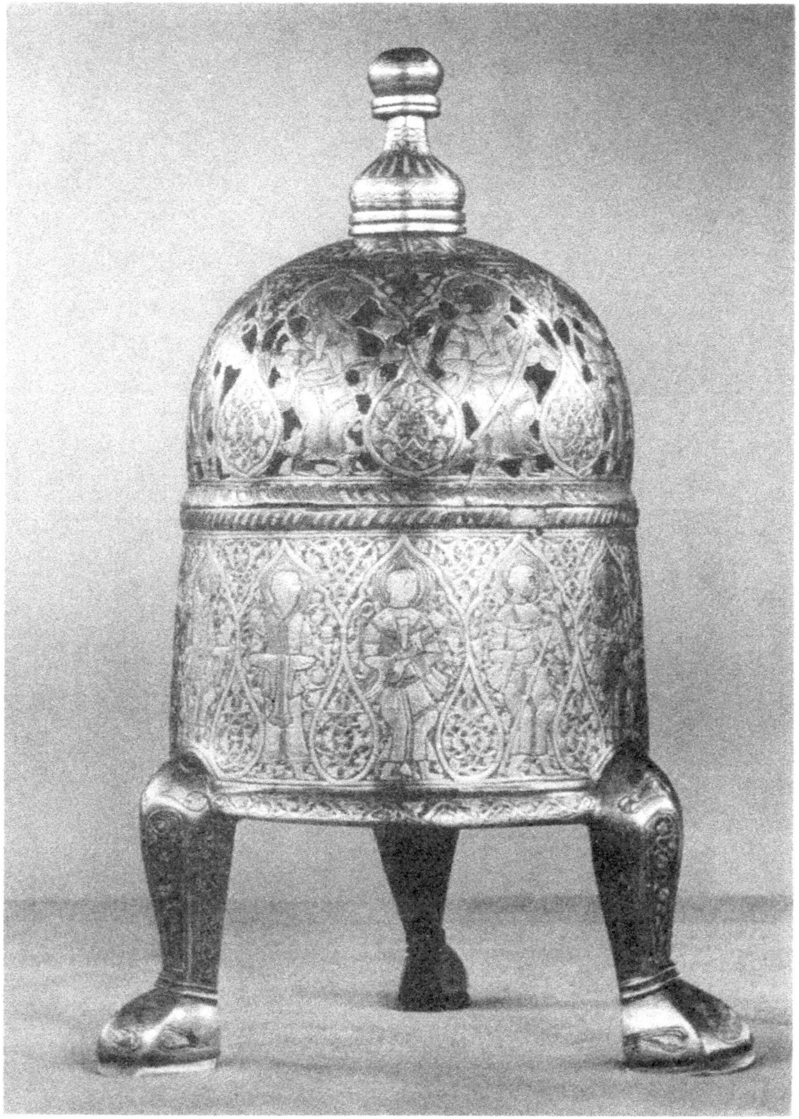

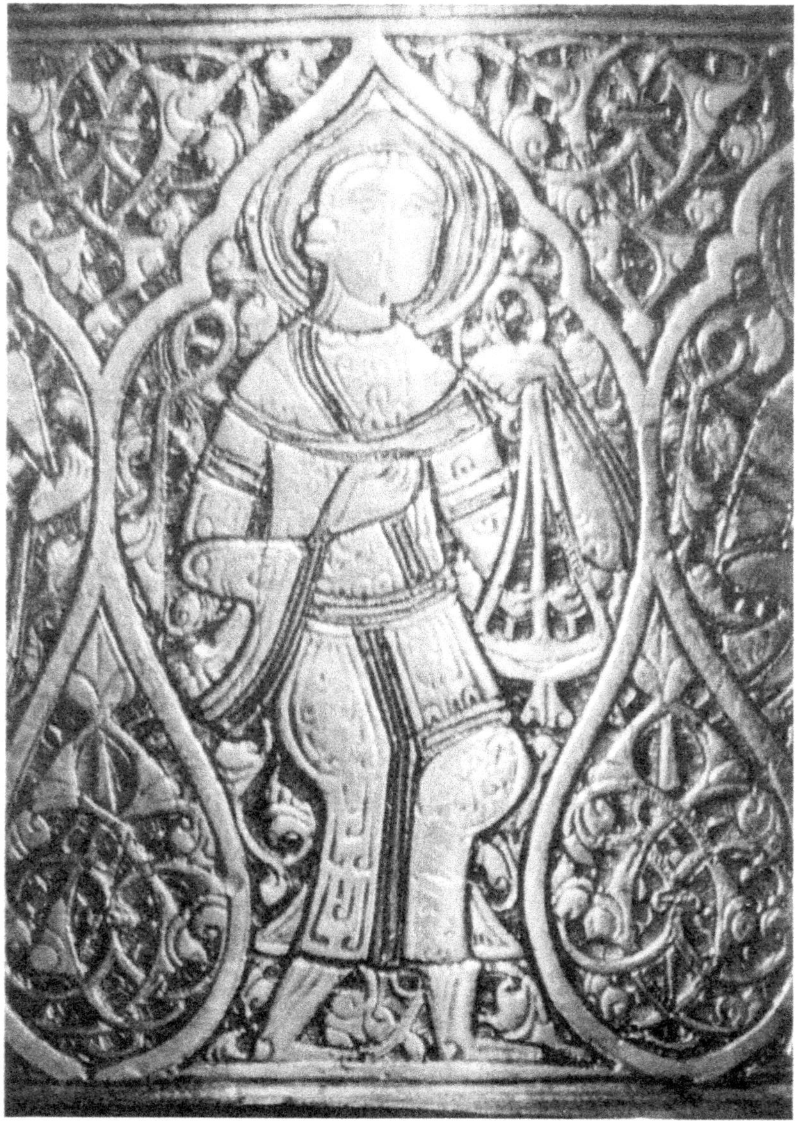

21(b). Detail.

21 (a)  Brass incense-burner, inlaid. *Syrian. Middle XIII Cent.*

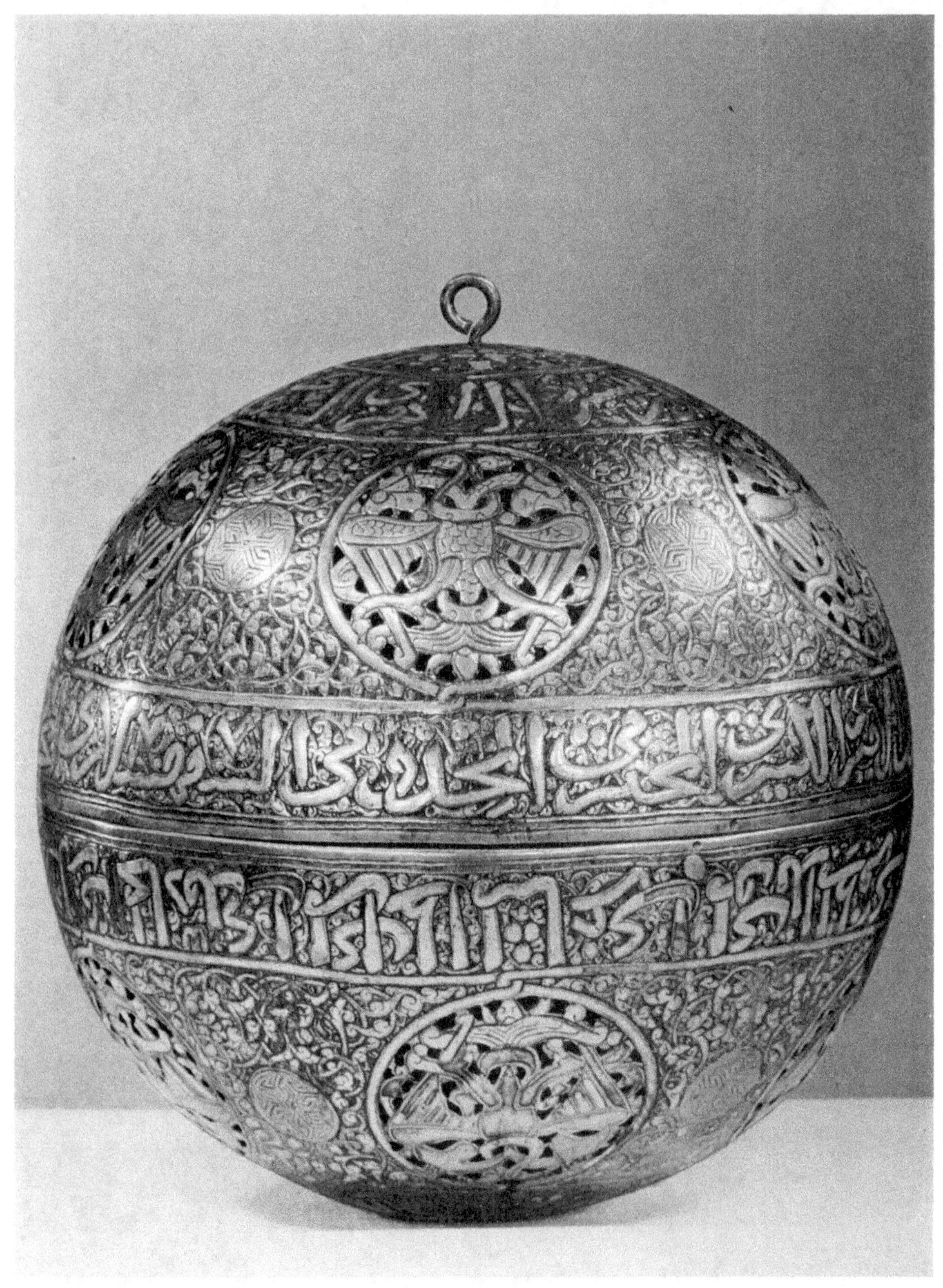

22. Brass handwarmer, inlaid. *Syrian.* 1264–79 *A.D.*

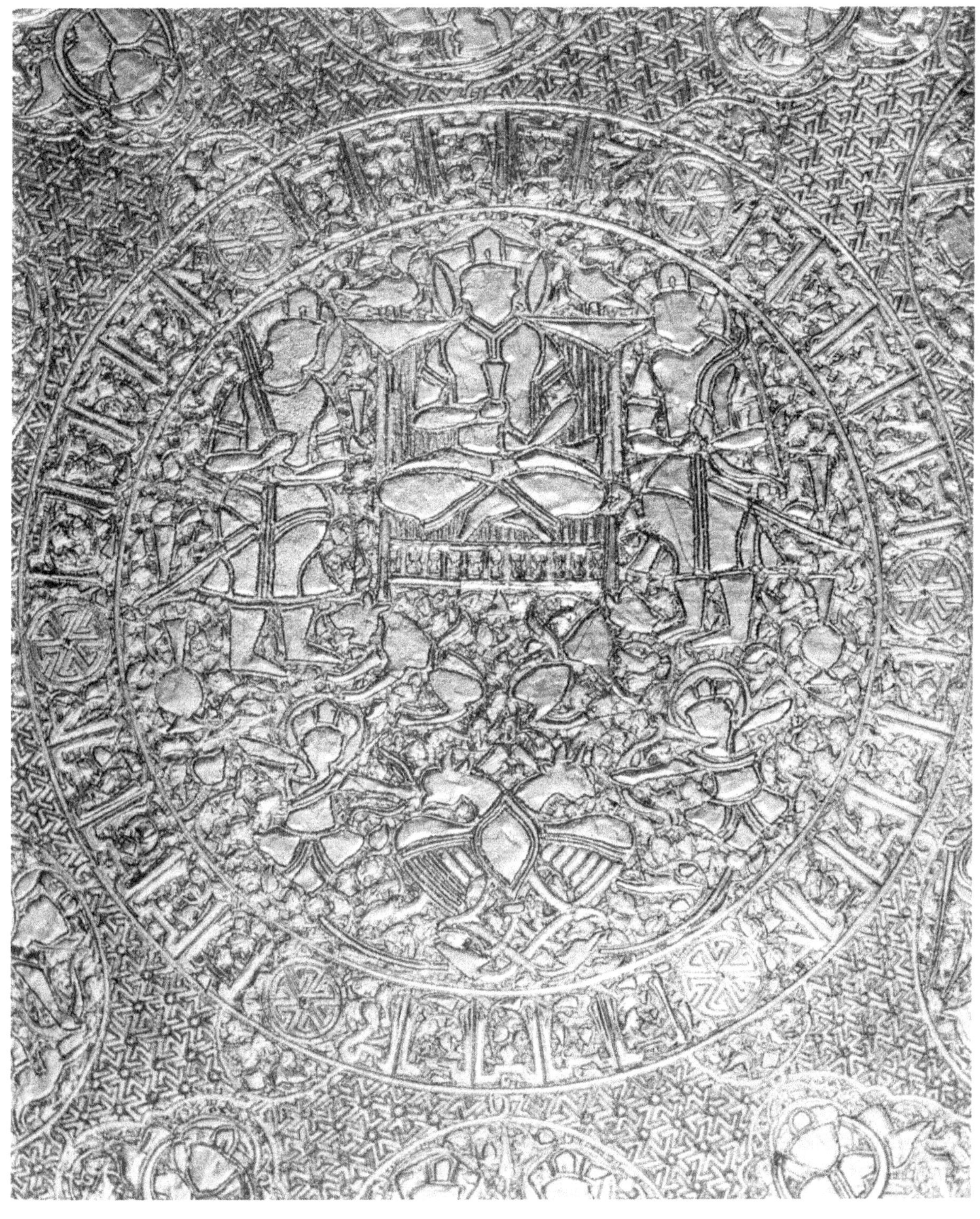

23. Detail of brass salver, inlaid. *Syrian. Second half of XIII Cent.*

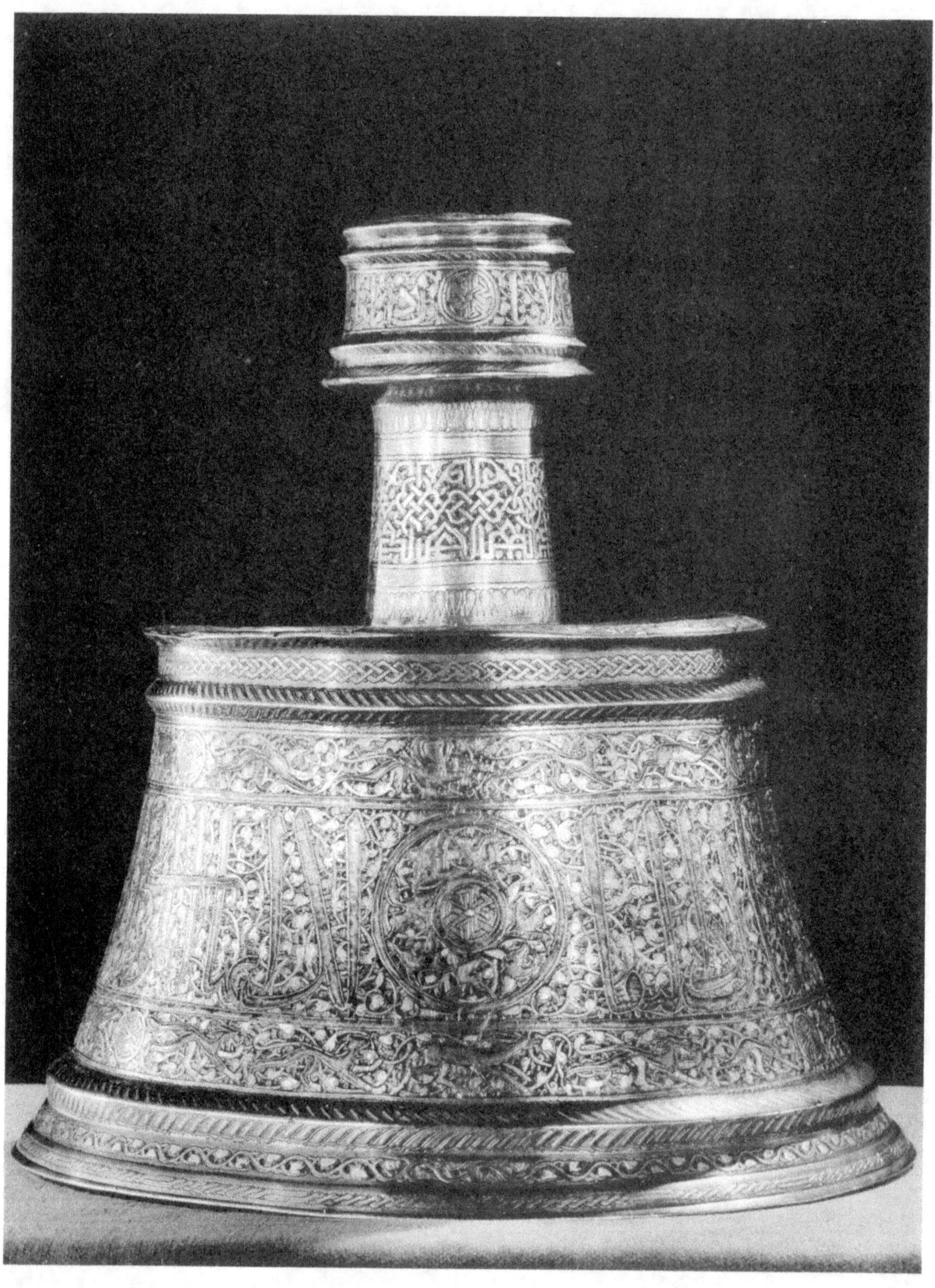

24. Brass candlestick, inlaid. *Syrian. Late XIII Cent.*

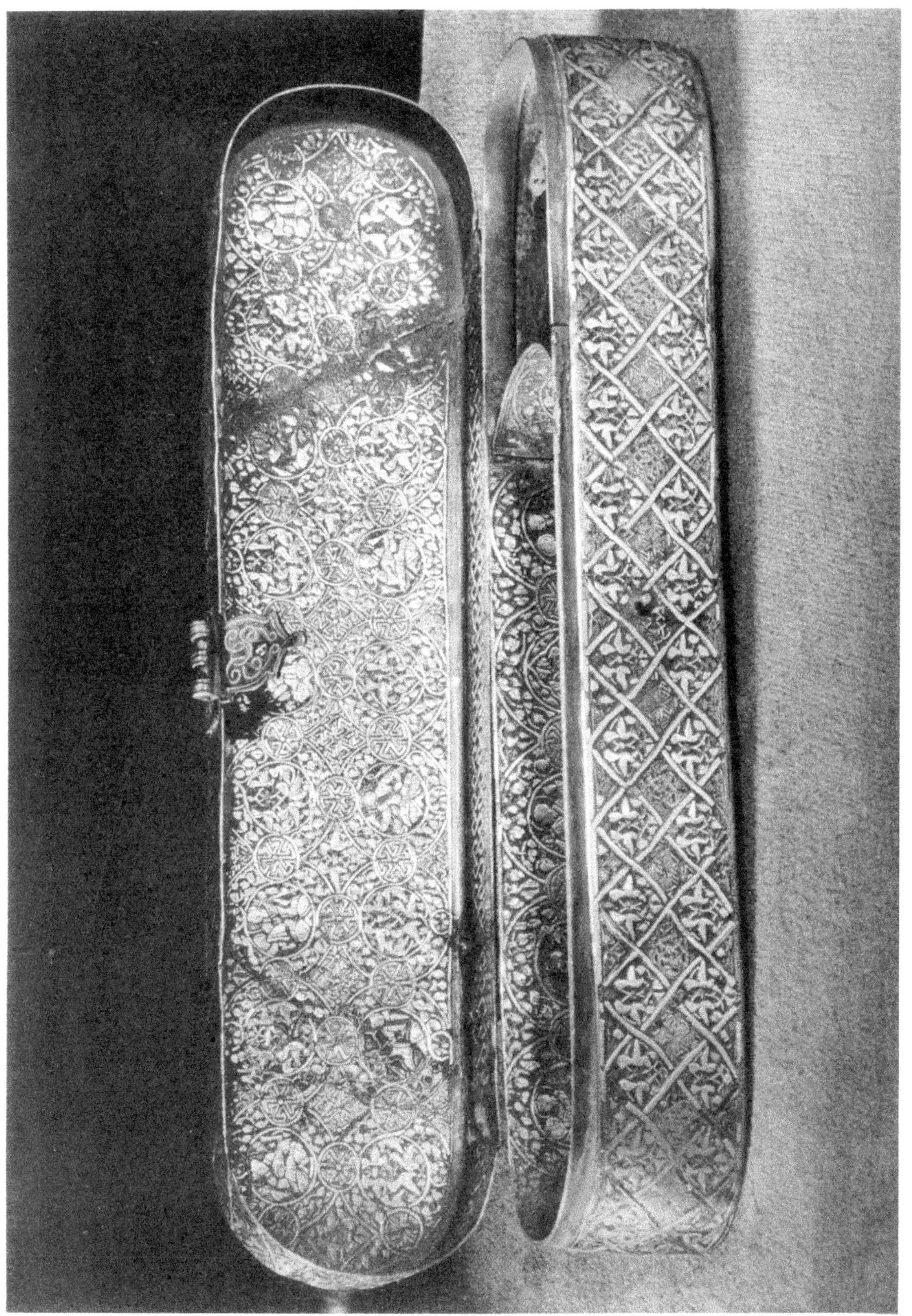

25. Brass writing box, inlaid. *Syrian. First half XIV Cent.*

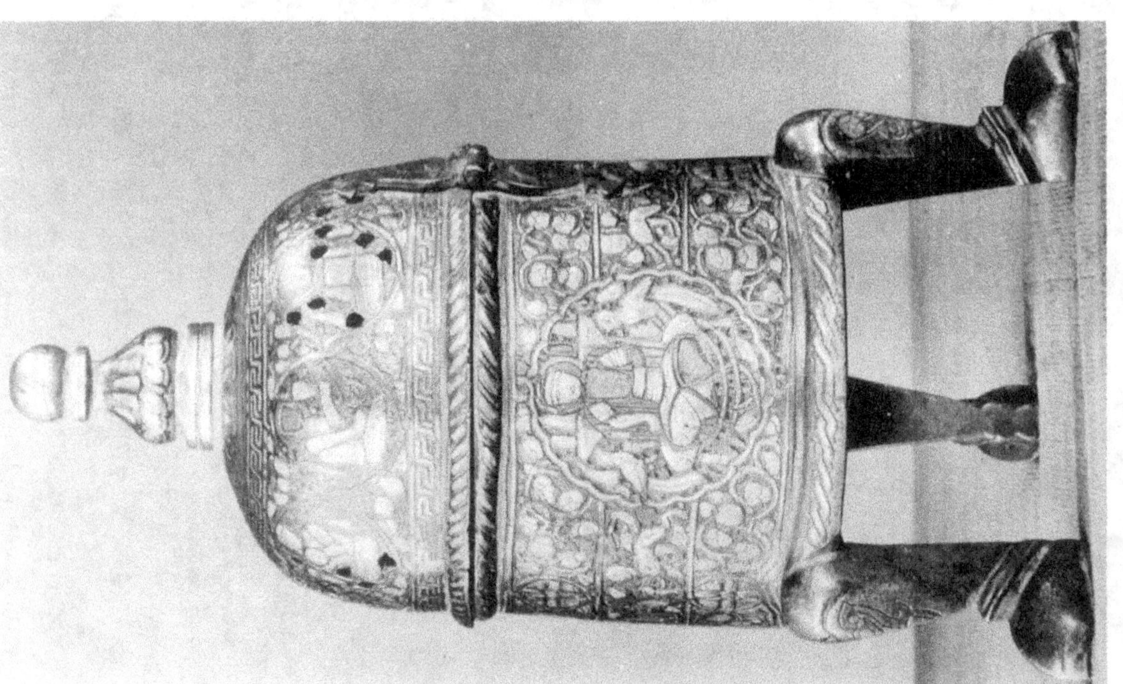

26(a). Brass incense-burner, inlaid. *Syrian. First half XIV Cent.*

26(b). Brass box, inlaid. *Egyptian. Early XIV Cent.*

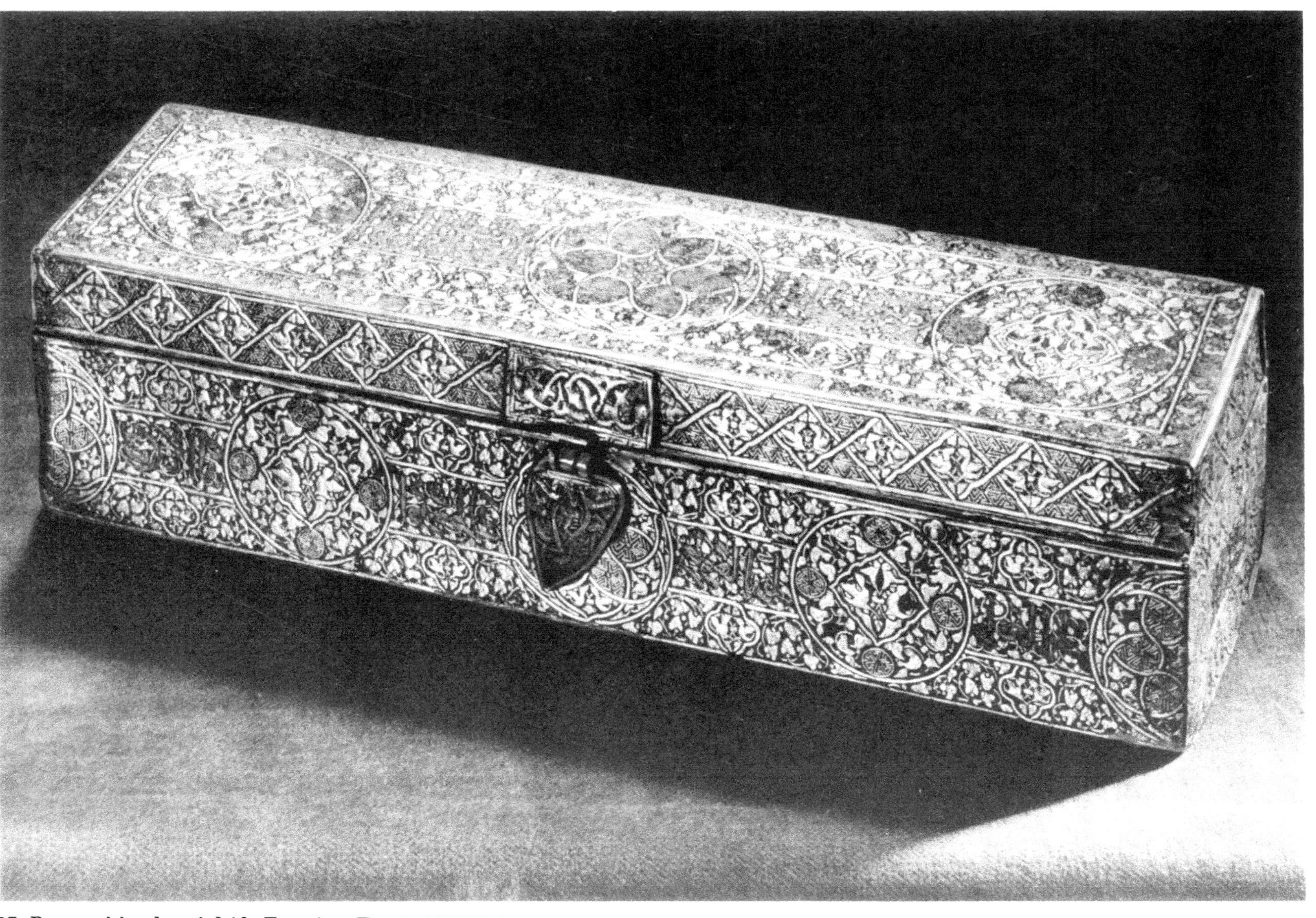

27. Brass writing box, inlaid. *Egyptian. First half XIV Cent.*

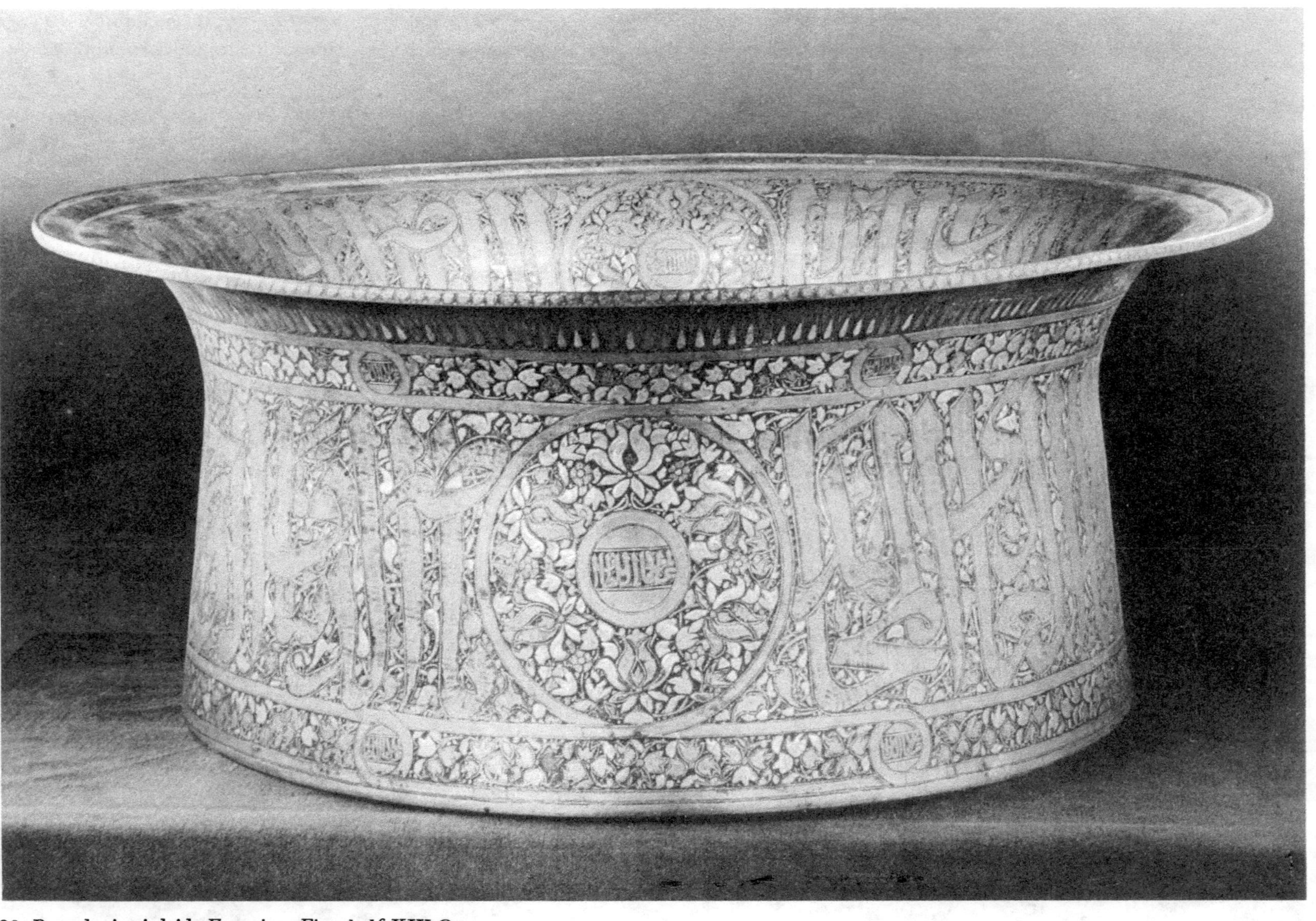

28. Brass basin, inlaid. *Egyptian. First half XIV Cent.*

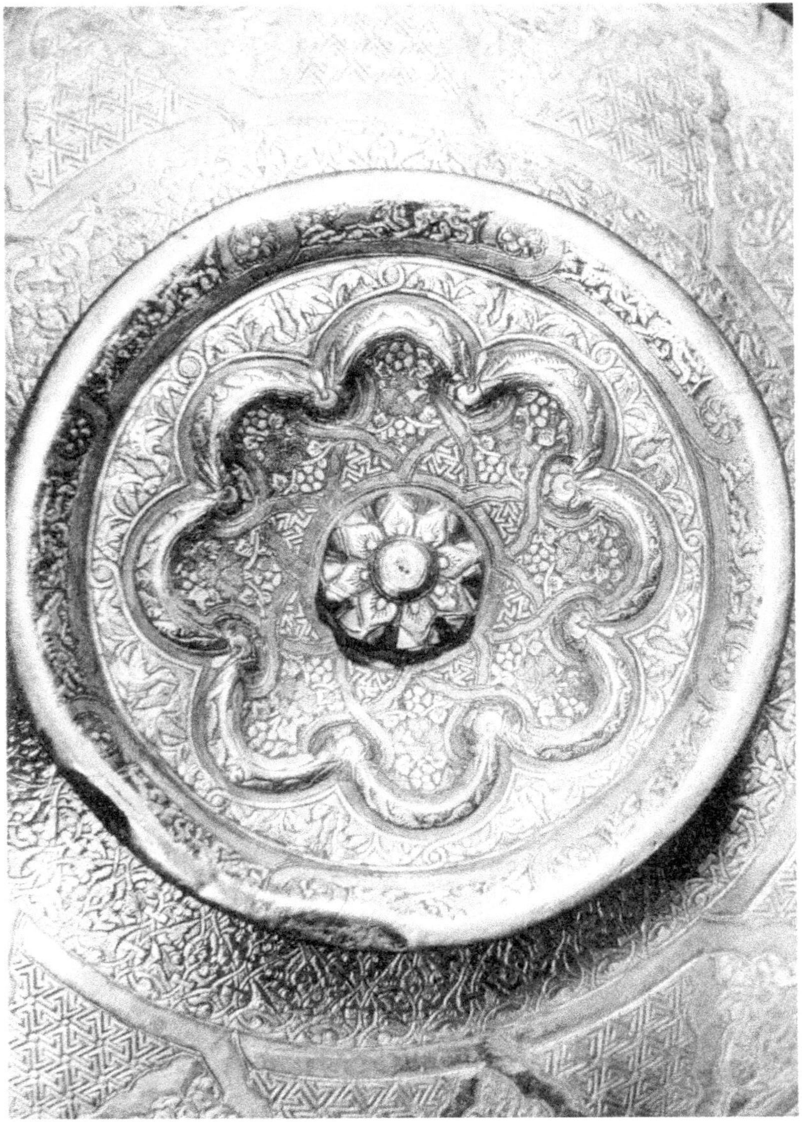

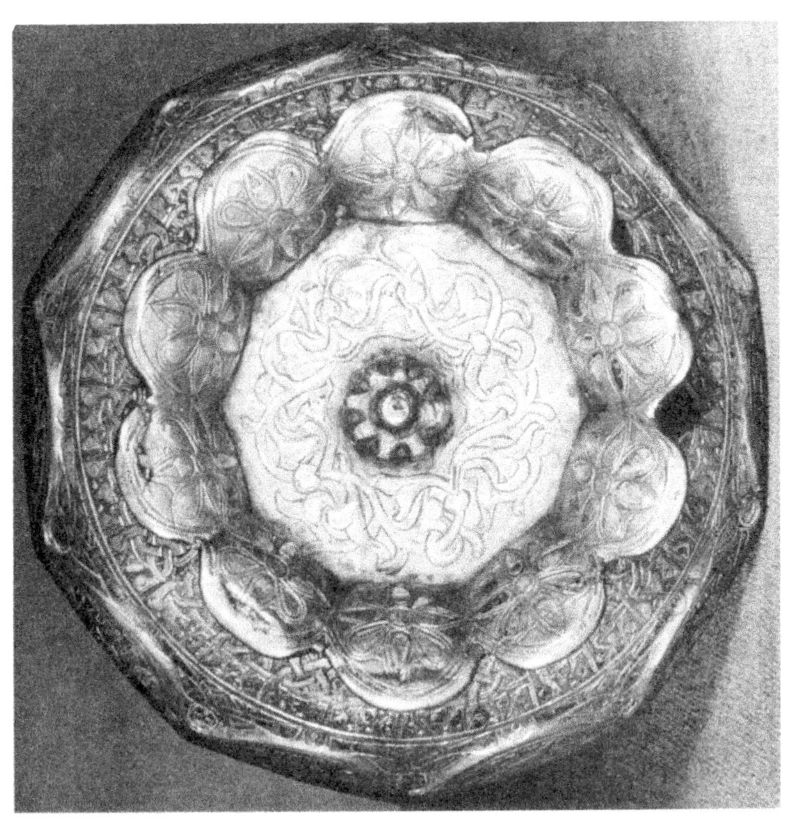

29(a). Base of vase on Plate 8.

29(b). Base of brass ewer, inlaid. *Egyptian. First half XIV Cent.*

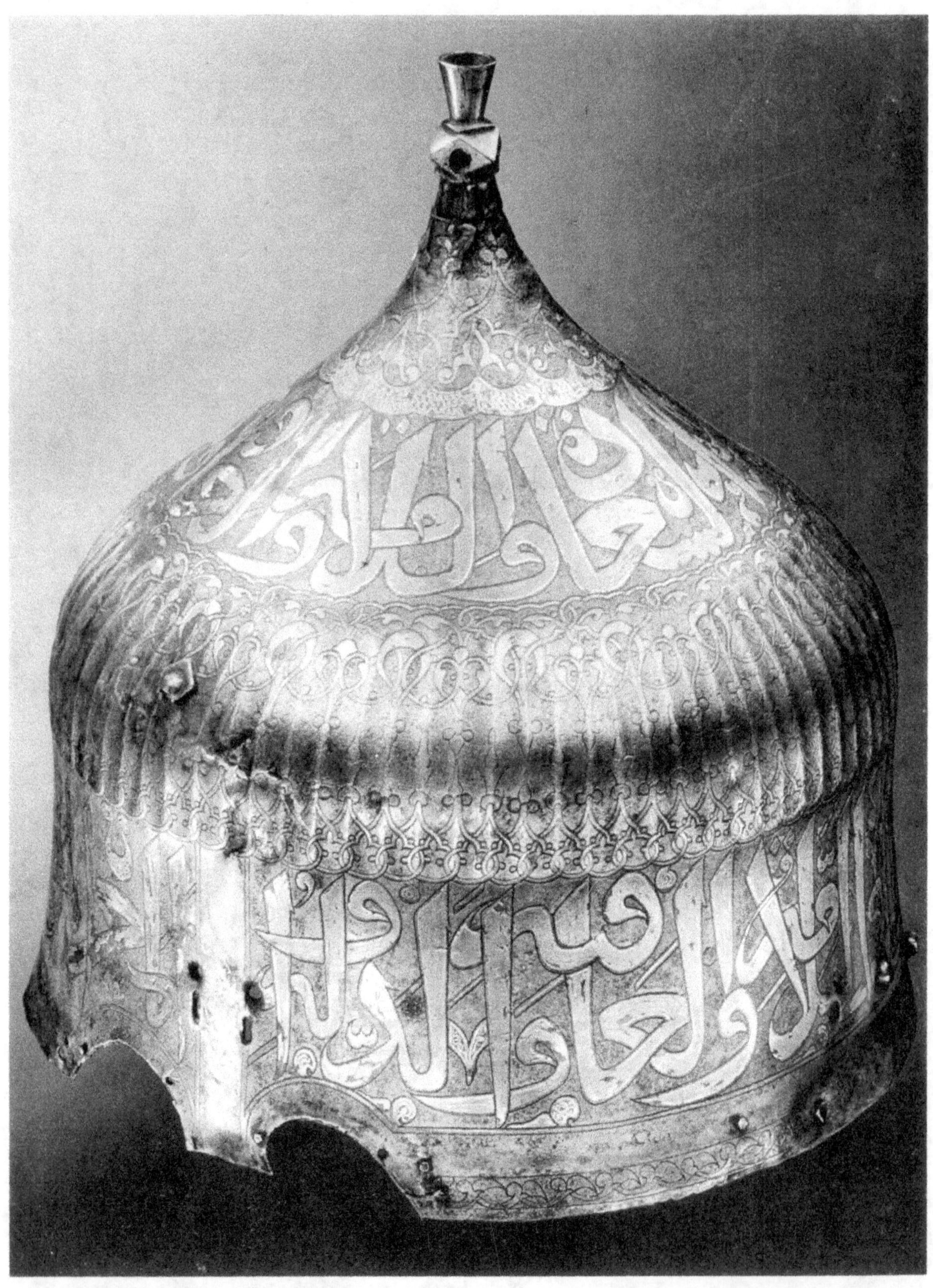

30. Steel helmet, gilt and inlaid. *Egyptian. XV Cent.*

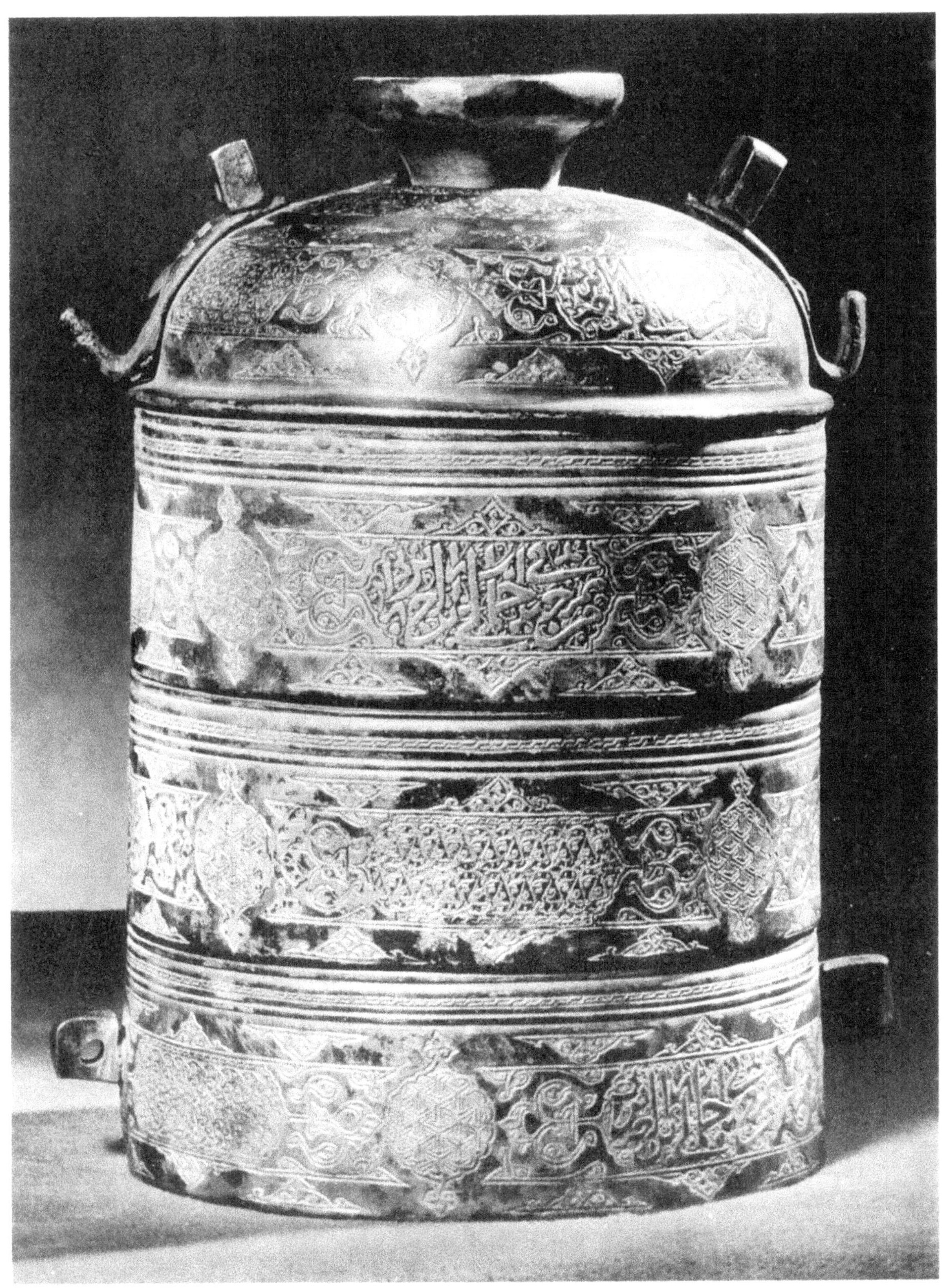

31. Brass food-box. *Egyptian. XVI Cent.*

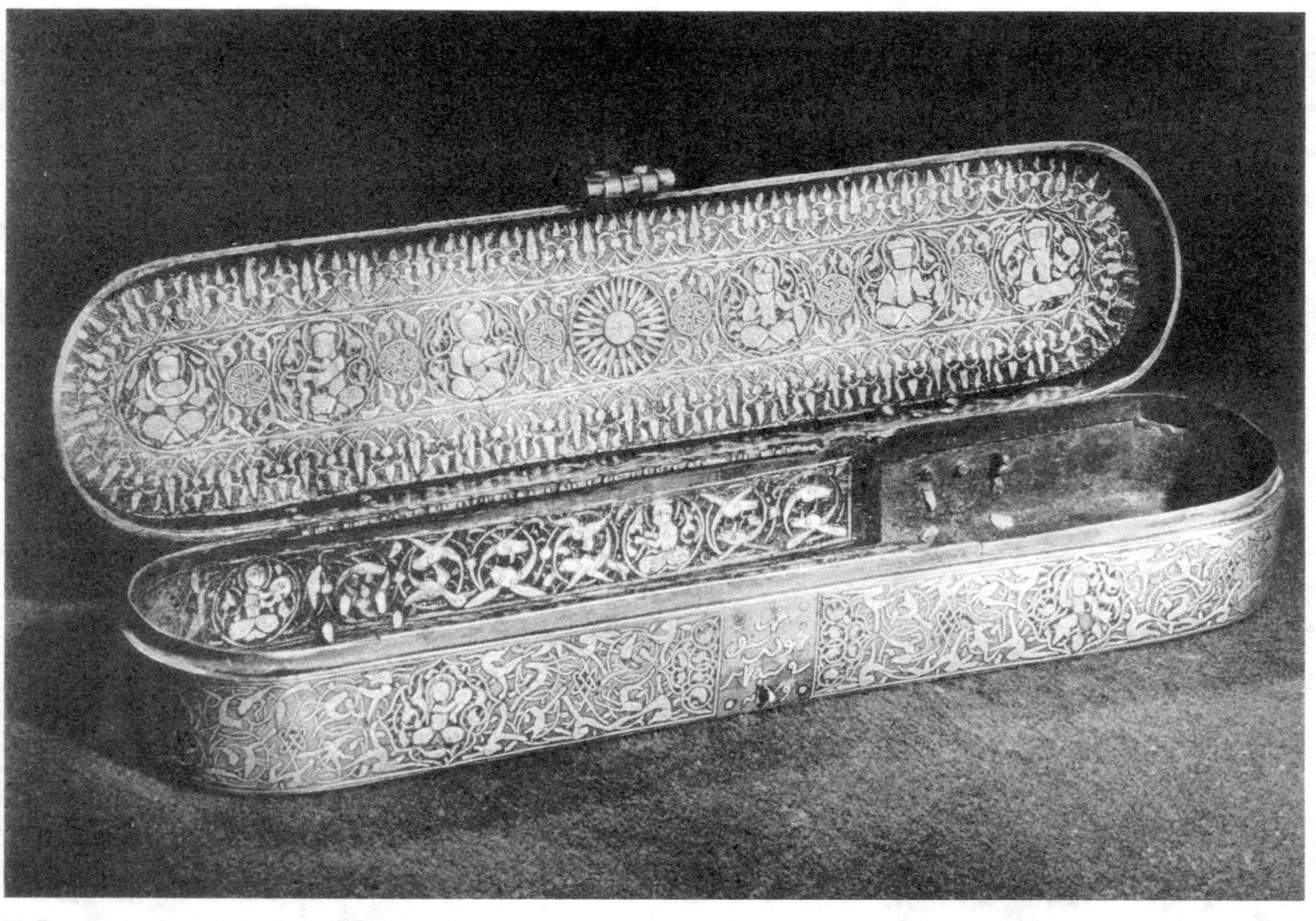

32. Brass writing box, inlaid. *Persian*(?). 1281 *A.D.*

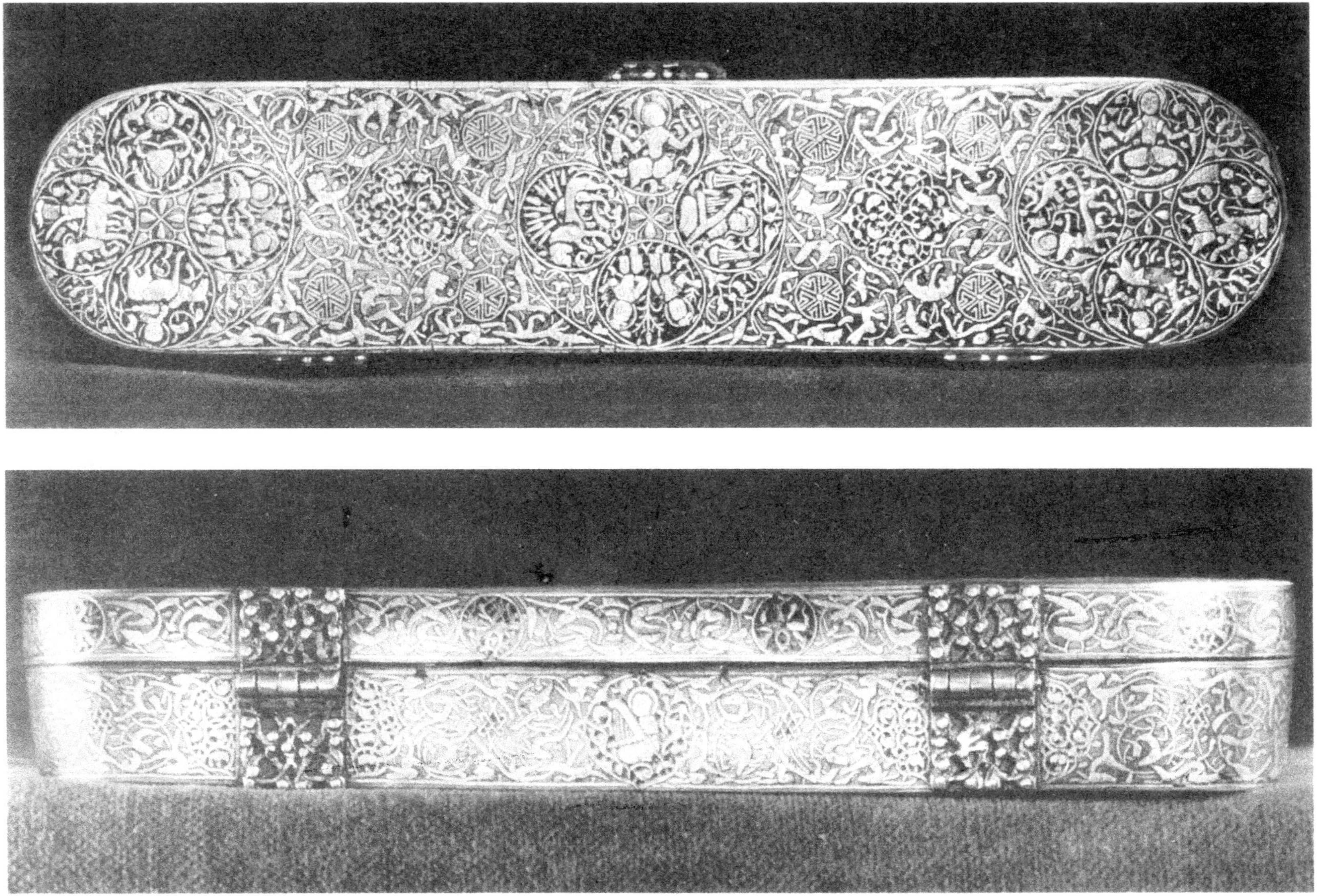

33. Top and side of writing box on Plate 32

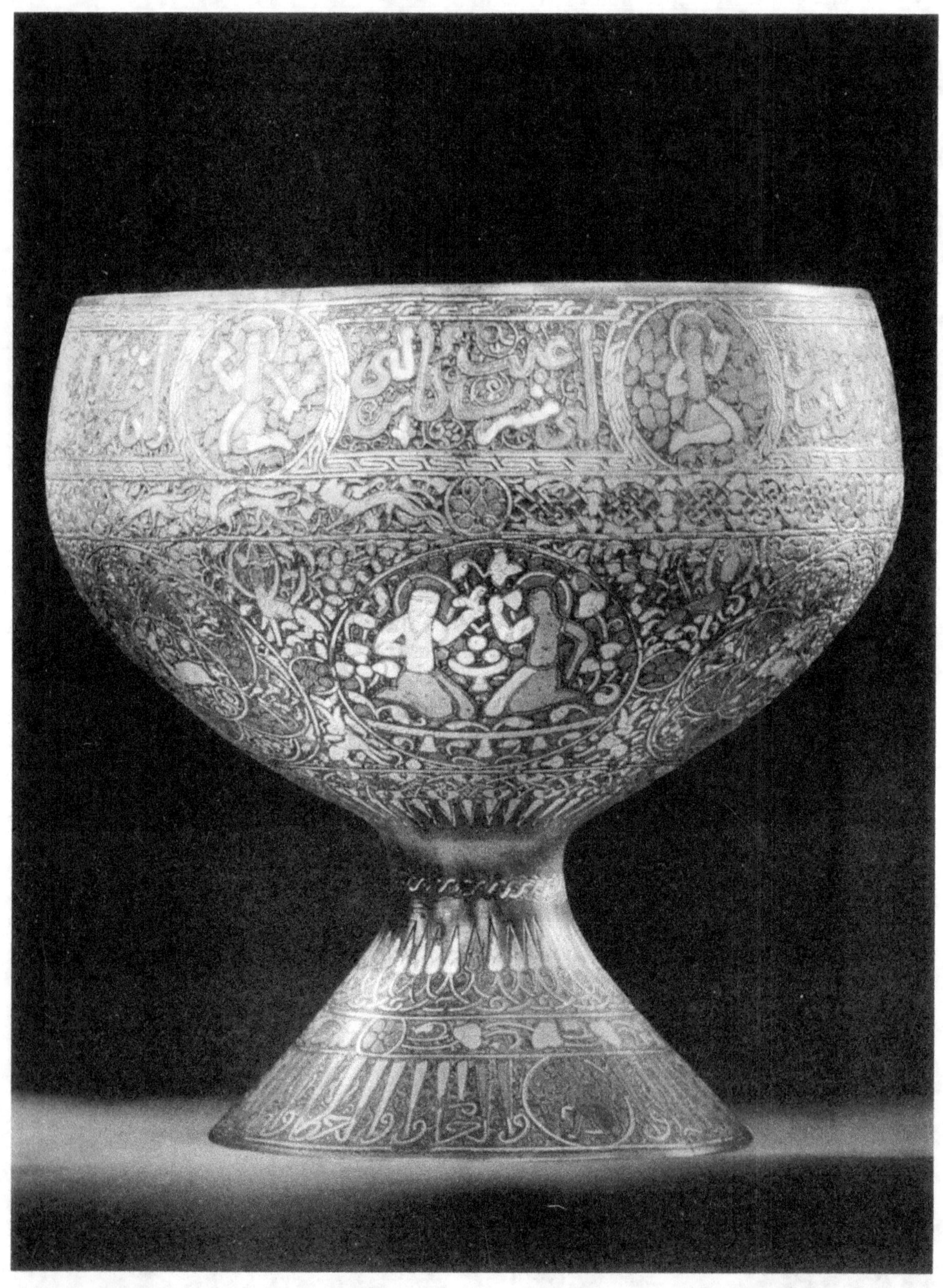

34. Brass goblet, inlaid. *Persian. XIV Cent.*

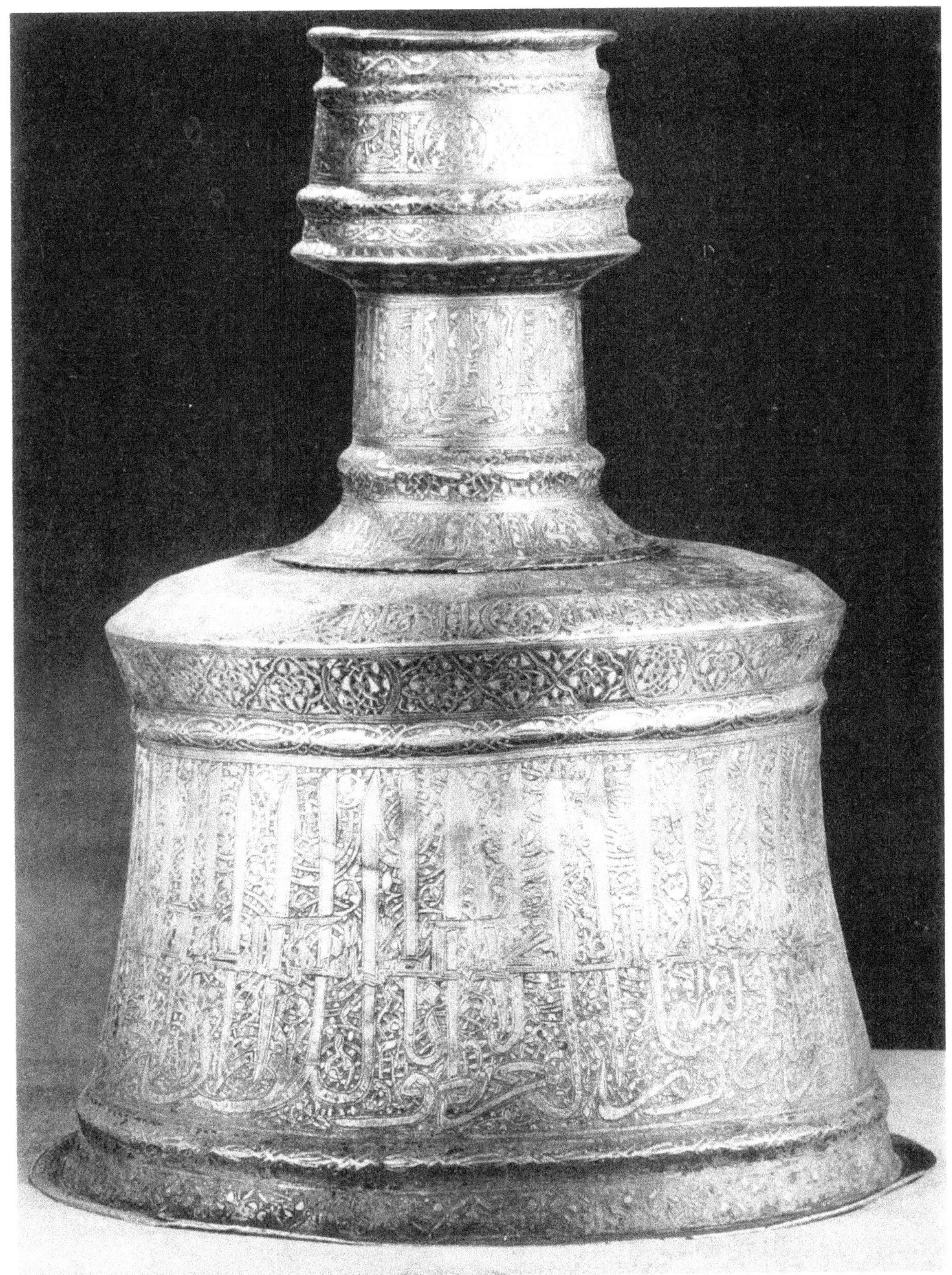

35. Brass candlestick, inlaid. *Persian. XIV Cent.*

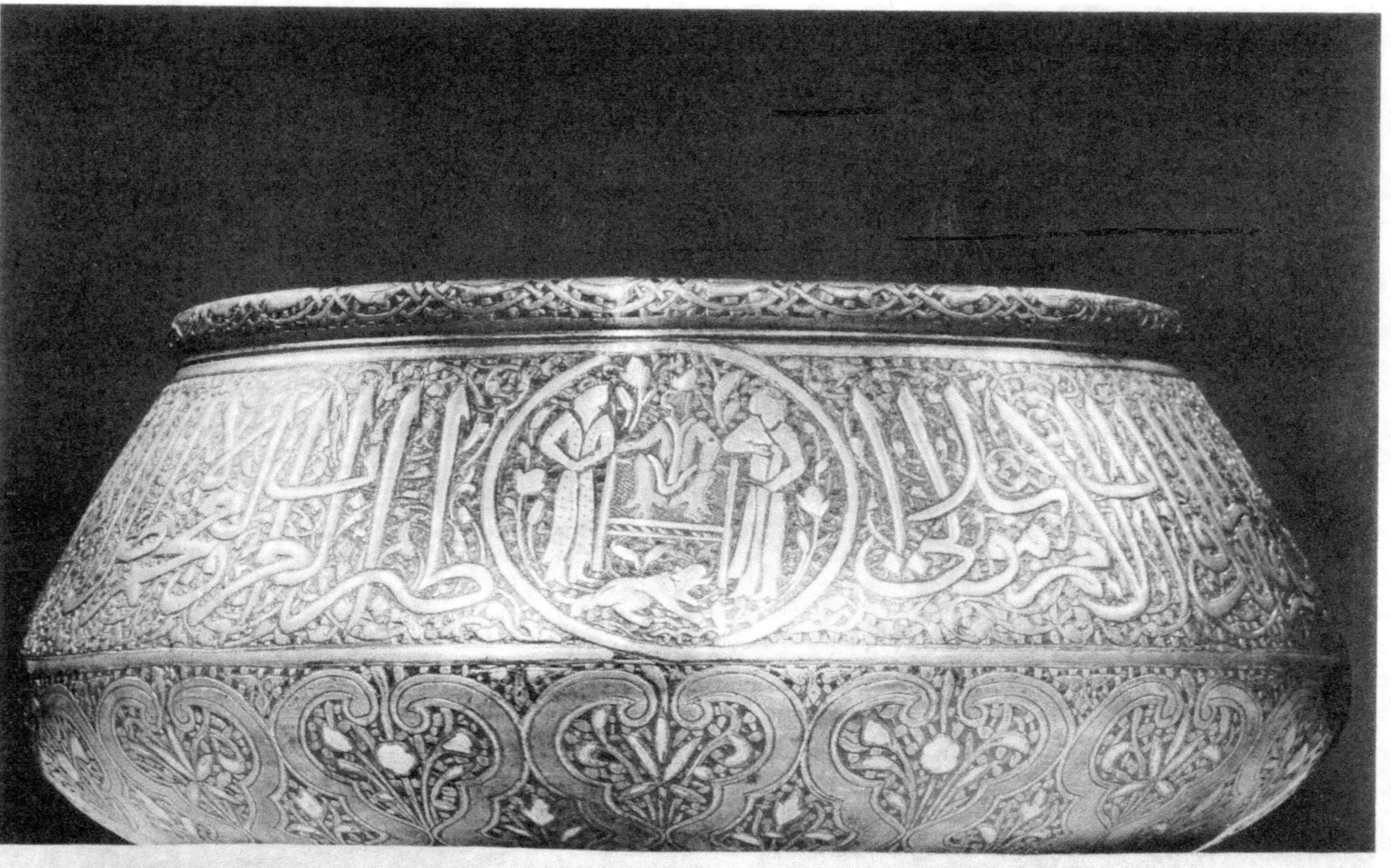

36. Brass bowl, inlaid. *Persian. Late XIV Cent.*

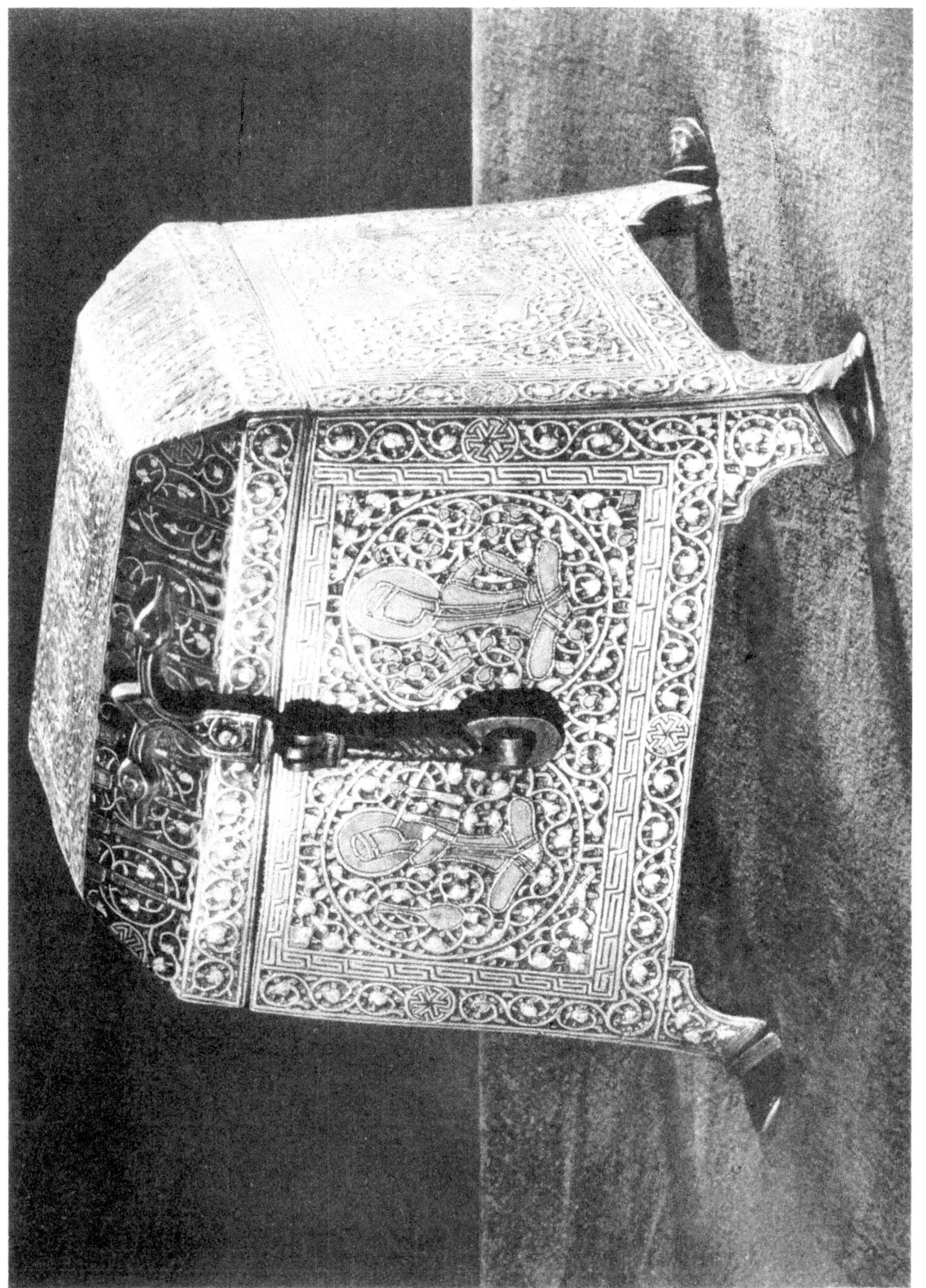

37. Brass casket, inlaid. *Persian. Late XIV Cent.*

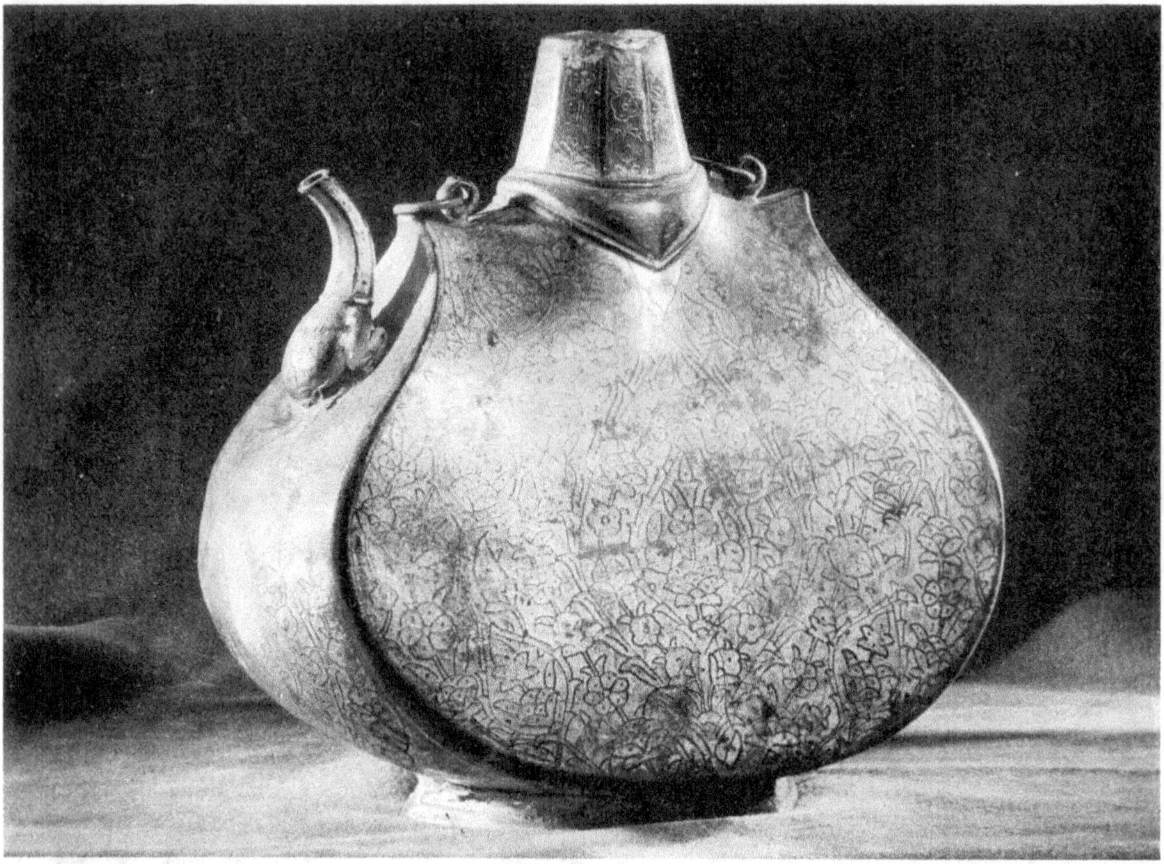

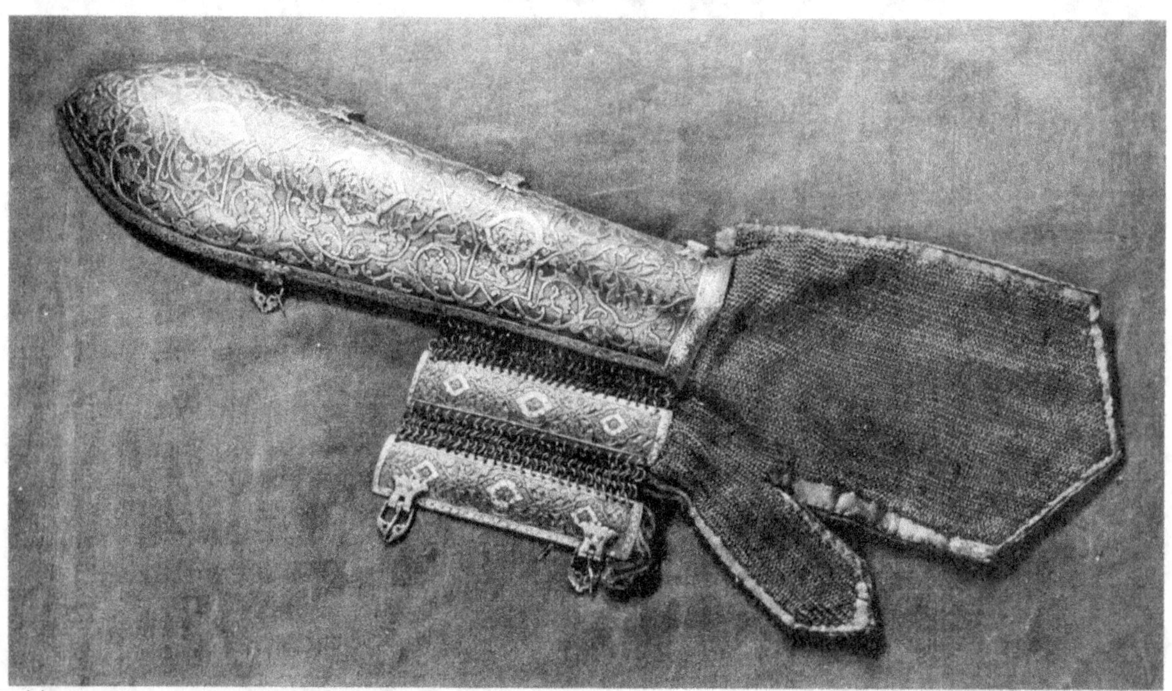

38(a). Copper ewer, gilt. *Persian. XVI Cent.*    38(b). Steel armpiece, inlaid. *Persian.* 1625–6 *A.D.*

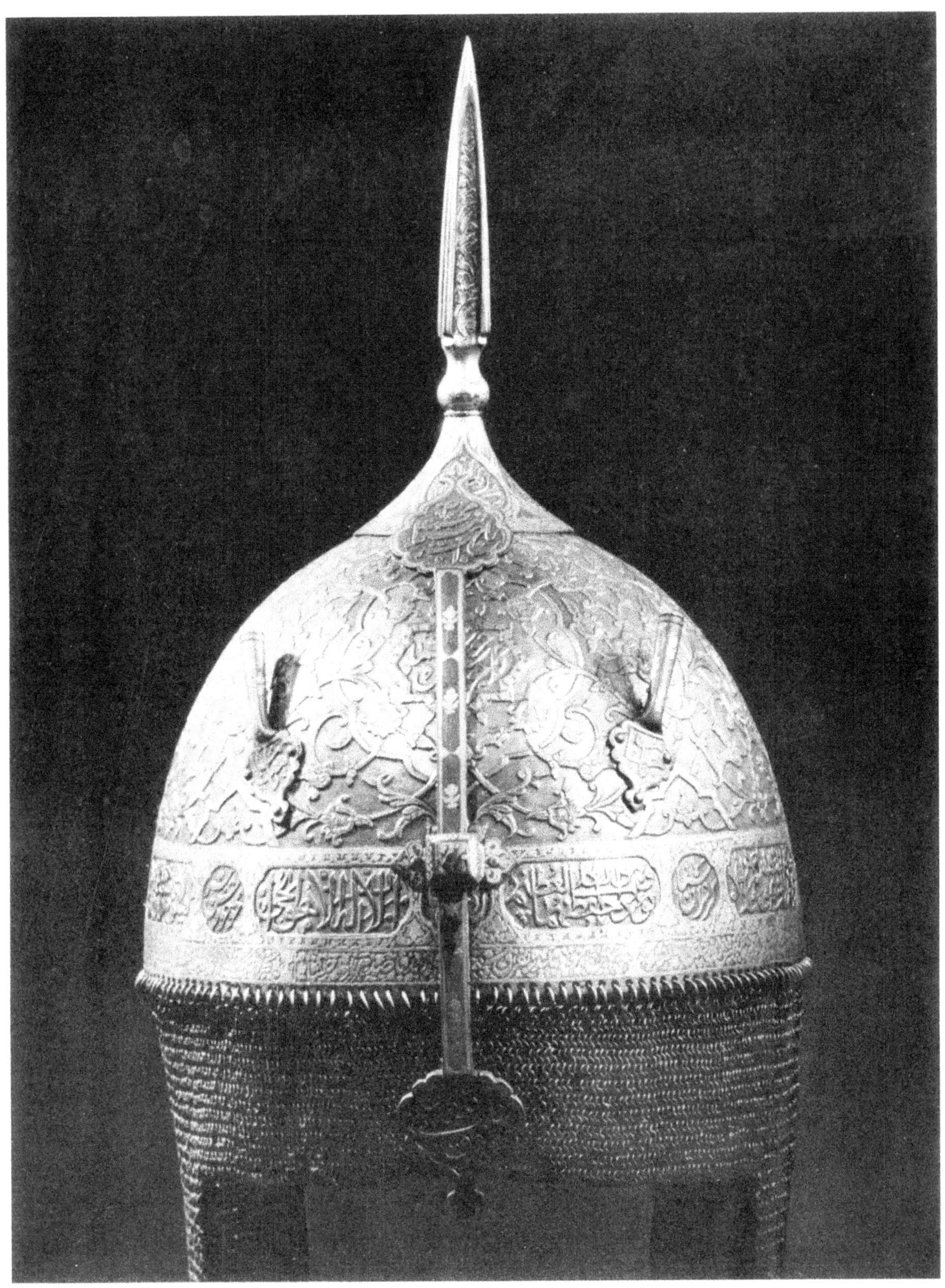

39. Steel helmet, inlaid. *Persian.* 1625–6 *A.D.*

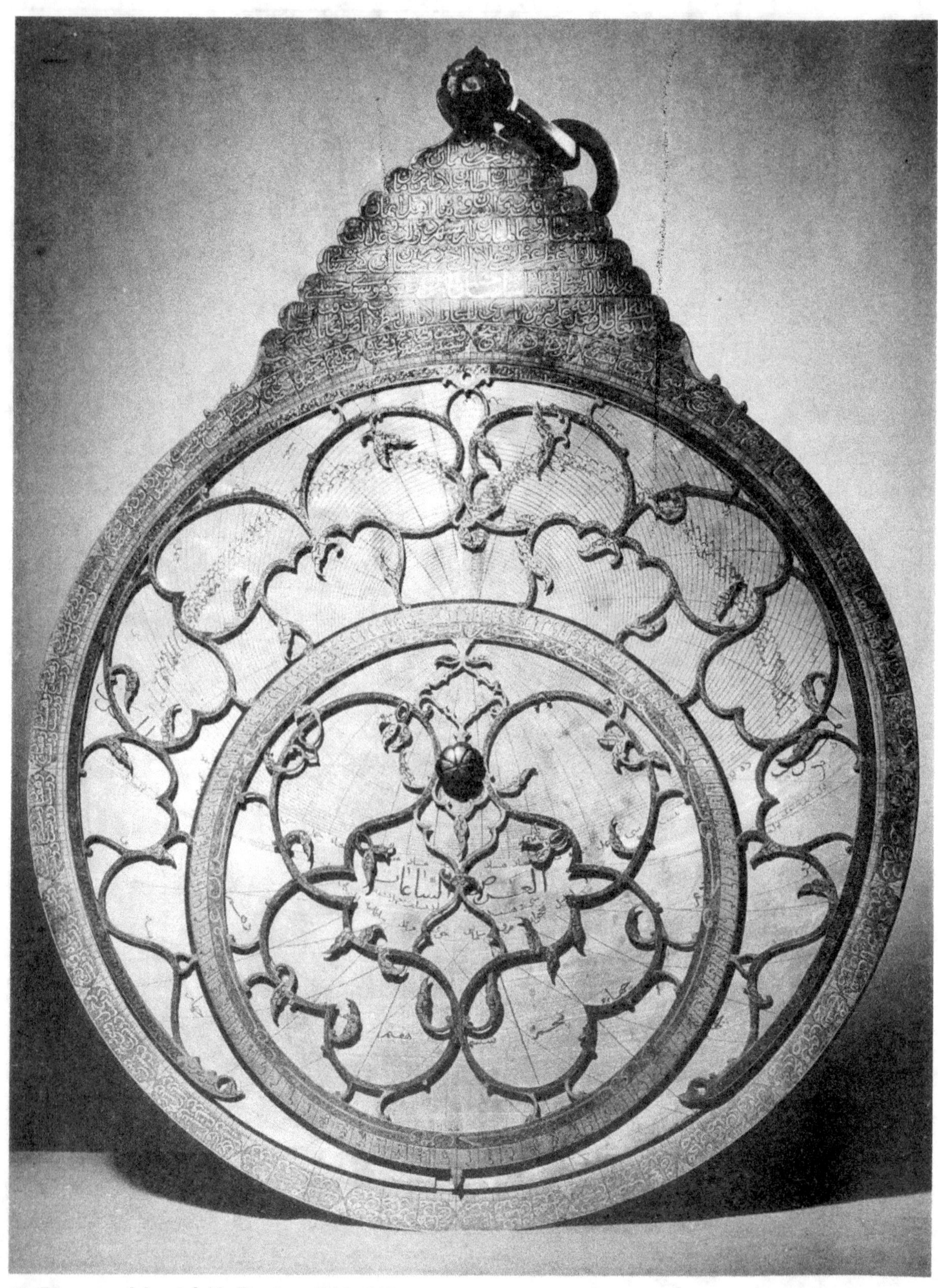

40. Brass astrolabe, inlaid. *Persian*. 1712 *A.D.*

For EU product safety concerns, contact us at Calle de José Abascal, 56–1°,
28003 Madrid, Spain or eugpsr@cambridge.org.